S. Hrg. 113–603

SYRIA SPILLOVER: THE GROWING THREAT OF TERRORISM AND SECTARIANISM IN THE MIDDLE EAST AND UKRAINE UPDATE

HEARING

BEFORE THE

COMMITTEE ON FOREIGN RELATIONS
UNITED STATES SENATE

ONE HUNDRED THIRTEENTH CONGRESS

SECOND SESSION

MARCH 6, 2014

Printed for the use of the Committee on Foreign Relations

Available via the World Wide Web: http://www.gpo.gov/fdsys/

U.S. GOVERNMENT PUBLISHING OFFICE

93–842 PDF   WASHINGTON : 2015

For sale by the Superintendent of Documents, U.S. Government Publishing Office
Internet: bookstore.gpo.gov   Phone: toll free (866) 512–1800; DC area (202) 512–1800
Fax: (202) 512–2104   Mail: Stop IDCC, Washington, DC 20402–0001

COMMITTEE ON FOREIGN RELATIONS

ROBERT MENENDEZ, New Jersey, *Chairman*

BARBARA BOXER, California
BENJAMIN L. CARDIN, Maryland
JEANNE SHAHEEN, New Hampshire
CHRISTOPHER A. COONS, Delaware
RICHARD J. DURBIN, Illinois
TOM UDALL, New Mexico
CHRISTOPHER MURPHY, Connecticut
TIM KAINE, Virginia
EDWARD J. MARKEY, Massachusetts

BOB CORKER, Tennessee
JAMES E. RISCH, Idaho
MARCO RUBIO, Florida
RON JOHNSON, Wisconsin
JEFF FLAKE, Arizona
JOHN McCAIN, Arizona
JOHN BARRASSO, Wyoming
RAND PAUL, Kentucky

DANIEL E. O'BRIEN, *Staff Director*
LESTER E. MUNSON III, *Republican Staff Director*

(II)

CONTENTS

(III)

SYRIA SPILLOVER: THE GROWING THREAT OF TERRORISM AND SECTARIANISM IN THE MIDDLE EAST AND UKRAINE UPDATE

THURSDAY, MARCH 6, 2014

U.S. SENATE,
COMMITTEE ON FOREIGN RELATIONS,
Washington, DC.

The committee met, pursuant to notice, at 11:07 a.m,. in room SD–419, Dirksen Senate Office Building, Hon. Robert Menendez (chairman of the committee) presiding.

Present: Senators Menendez, Cardin, Shaheen, Murphy, Kaine, Markey, Corker, Risch, Johnson, Flake, Barrasso, and Paul.

OPENING STATEMENT OF HON. ROBERT MENENDEZ, U.S. SENATOR FROM NEW JERSEY

The CHAIRMAN. This hearing will come to order. Let me thank Deputy Secretary of State Burns for coming. While this was planned, obviously, well before the current state of events, understanding the challenges of your schedule, we appreciate your still being here today with us, as well as all of our panelists for being here to provide their perspective on the increasingly violent spillover from the ongoing conflict in Syria, and to hear also from the Deputy Secretary on the implication of Russia's military intervention in the Ukraine.

As a cautionary note, we have a vote that will be taking place at around 11:20. So we will see where we are at in the proceeding. We may have to recess briefly. It is one vote; to vote and then come back. I am sure the Deputy Secretary would be happy for us to cast that vote since it is about Rose Gottemoeller.

As we enter year 3 of the Syria crisis, headlines coming out of the region are no longer limited to the violence within Syria, but to the increasing spread of violence across Syria's borders, especially into Lebanon and Iraq. Of great concern is the proliferation of al-Qaeda affiliates and splinter groups and the increasing sectarian rhetoric fueling the increased violence that offers new opportunities for al-Qaeda to gain footholds in local communities.

It opens the door for an Iranian-sponsored terrorist network to justify their presence as the protector of the region's Shias, while bolstering the Assad regime and antagonizing Arab States.

The spillover from Syria is dangerous and troubling. In Lebanon there has been an alarming uptick in high-profile bombings, many claimed by the al-Qaeda-affiliated Abdullah Azam Brigades, and at the same time Hezbollah, purportedly protecting the Lebanese Shia communities, now extending into Syria, protecting the Assad regime.

From where I sit, the region is becoming increasingly unstable, increasingly violent, and increasingly sectarian. Having said that, that is a major challenge for which the committee obviously wanted to rivet our attention, Ukraine is the 800-pound gorilla at the moment and we cannot ignore it. Nor can we ignore that Russia is a common element in both countries. Russia's support for Assad in Syria and the Russian invasion and occupation of parts of Ukraine make clear that Putin's game is not 21st century statesmanship, but 19th century gamesmanship.

The brave protesters in Maidan Square, having lived under Russia's mantle for years, stood their ground because they understood that their fight was not just with their government's corrupt leaders, but also for the very future of their independent nation. Putin has cast aside both international law and his nation's own commitments to respect the territorial integrity of the Ukraine.

We need a policy that checks and counters Russia's self-centered, nationalistic and imperialistic, policy that adheres to no law, not international law, nor even those commitments it has made personally.

Today our concern is for the Ukraine. Tomorrow it again could be for Georgia or perhaps Moldova, two nations waiting to finalize their association agreement with the European Union, a process that the Ukraine was engaged in, to the displeasure of the Russian Government.

I want to note that I welcome the administration's expeditious response to the situation in Ukraine, the pledge of assistance in the form of loan guarantees, which this committee intends to endorse in legislation next week, and today's Executive order restricting visas, freezing assets, blocking property under U.S. jurisdiction, and preventing American companies from doing business with any individual or entity identified by the administration that threatens the peace, security, stability, sovereignty, or territorial integrity of Ukraine, or contributes to the misappropriation of state assets of the Ukraine, or purports to assert governmental authority over any part of Ukraine without authorization from the Ukrainian Government in Kiev.

This flexible tool will allow the United States to target those directly responsible for the Crimean crisis and will further put Putin and his allies on notice that Russia's actions are not without consequence. The committee is prepared to codify this action and potentially provide the President with further authority to respond to the situation as it develops.

President Putin's game of Russian roulette has pointed the gun at the international community's head. I believe this time he has miscalculated and I certainly believe it is essential that we do not blink. The unity of purpose displayed at the U.N. Security Council by the European Union and the G7 nations in support of Ukrainian autonomy, and in opposition to Russian authoritarianism, demonstrates the world's outrage, and I believe serves as a call to action.

With that, I would be happy to recognize the distinguished ranking Republican, Senator Corker, for his remarks.

OPENING STATEMENT OF HON. BOB CORKER,
U.S. SENATOR FROM TENNESSEE

Senator CORKER. Thank you, Mr. Chairman, and thank you for having this hearing, and thank you for allowing it to evolve from Syria to Ukraine because of the current events. I want to thank all of you for your public service and for being here. I know that you do not necessarily decide what the policy is, but you carry it out. I just want to say that I could not be more disappointed in where we are in Syria. It is kind of amazing how prognosticators, both here on this panel, at the dais here, and around the world, stated what was going to happen in Syria over time if we did not change the balance on the ground, and unfortunately that is exactly what has happened.

It has turned into a regional conflict, destabilizing other countries. Al-Qaeda is on the rise, not only, and other extremists, in Syria, where our Director of National Intelligence and others are now stating this is becoming a threat to the homeland, but it is also a threat to the entire region. You can witness that on the ground in Iraq now, this incredible violence that is occurring there, and as the chairman just mentioned, in Lebanon.

You know, we tried to help the administration by passing something here in this committee and we did so on a 15–3 vote to arm and really support the vetted opposition. Unfortunately, the administration just never came around to doing the things that it stated publicly that it would do, and it just never has done it. So this has festered and there has never been a change that has caused Assad to really even want to sit down and negotiate. Obviously, what happened at Geneva 2 is what everybody expected.

We gave the President, out of committee on a 10–7 vote, the authorization for the use of force, and yet the President really not only did not really make a case for it publicly, but obviously sort of jumped in Russia's lap to help us out of this situation in the deal with chemical weapons. Since then I know that 30 to 40,000 people have been killed. I do not know if the people who have been killed really care whether it was through chemical weapons or through barrel bombs that are being indiscriminately dropped on civilians right now. But it is a disaster of great proportions.

It is certainly a failure on our part and many other nations relative to foreign policy, and it is destabilizing the region. I could not be more disappointed.

And the two are related, as the chairman just mentioned. I do not know that we could say that Russia would not have done what it did in Ukraine with a different approach. I do not think we can state that. But I think that the permissive environment that we have created through this reset, thinking that someone like Putin reacts to warmth and charm and reach-out, when what he really reacts to is weakness and I think he has seen that in our foreign policy efforts over the course of this last year.

Again, I do not think we can make a case that what happened in Crimea would not have happened, but I certainly do not think he has felt that there would be much of a pushback from us.

So I am thankful today that, again, there are some steps that are being taken. As the chairman mentioned, we stand ready, here, to enable the administration to act even more forcefully. We had a great meeting yesterday. But I could not be more disappointed that we are where we are. I think our credibility very much has been on the line, is on the line, and I do think that us having a unified and very strong reaction and approach over a long time, not something that is just short-term, over a long time, is very important relative to Russia right now, as is regaining some of that credibility.

So I thank you for being here. I know you are going to talk some about Syria. I hope you will explain more fully what you think these sanctions that have been announced this morning are about. I think that would be helpful to us over the next few days in doing something that is complementary to those efforts. So I thank you for being here, and I thank you, Mr. Chairman.

The CHAIRMAN. Thank you, Senator Corker.

We will start off with Deputy Secretary Burns, who also served as Ambassador to Russia from 2005 to 2008 and has some obvious firsthand experience. We also are pleased to have with us the Assistant Secretary of Defense for International Security Affairs, Derek Chollet. We appreciate you being here, as well as the Director for the National Counterterrorism Center, Matt Olsen. We thank you all.

All of your statements will be fully included in the record without objection, and I would ask you to more or less summarize within 5 minutes. If you go over a little bit, obviously with the gravity of the situation we want to hear from you. But I know that members do want to engage in a conversation with you about their issues and concerns.

With that, Mr. Secretary, you are recognized.

STATEMENT OF HON. WILLIAM J. BURNS, DEPUTY SECRETARY OF STATE, U.S. DEPARTMENT OF STATE, WASHINGTON, DC

Ambassador BURNS. Thank you very much, Chairman Menendez, Ranking Member Corker, members of the committee. I very much appreciate this opportunity. I am pleased to be joined by Matt Olsen and Derek Chollet and I appreciate your putting my written testimony into the record.

Before addressing the issue of extremism in the Levant, let me first offer a quick assessment of developments in Ukraine, as you requested. A great deal is at stake in Ukraine today. Less than 48 hours ago, in Kiev not far from the Shrine of the Fallen, Secretary Kerry made clear America's deep and abiding commitment to Ukraine's sovereignty and territorial integrity in the face of Russian aggression and our determination to ensure that the people of Ukraine get to make their own choices about their future. That is the bedrock conviction for the United States.

On my own visit last week, I was profoundly moved by the bravery and selflessness of Ukrainians and profoundly impressed by the commitment of the new interim government to reach across ethnic and regional lines and build a stable, democratic, and inclusive Ukraine with good relations with all of its neighbors, including Russia.

While we and our partners worked to support Ukraine's transition, Russia worked actively to undermine it. Russia's military intervention in Crimea is a brazen violation of its international obligations and no amount of Russian posturing can obscure that fact. Ukraine's interim government, approved by 82 percent of the Rada, including most members of Yanukovych's party, has shown admirable restraint in the face of massive provocation. They need and deserve our strong support.

President Obama, Secretary Kerry, and the entire administration have been working hard, steadily, and methodically, to build urgent international backing for Ukraine, counterpressure against Russia, reassurance to other neighbors, and a path to deescalation. Our strategy has four main elements, and we look forward to working with this committee and with the Congress on each of them.

First, immediate support for Ukraine as it deals with enormous economic challenges and prepares for critical national elections at the end of May. On Tuesday Secretary Kerry announced our intent to seek a $1 billion loan guarantee. That will be part of a major international effort to build a strong economic support package for Ukraine as it undertakes reform. That effort includes the IMF and the EU, which laid out its own substantial assistance package yesterday.

Prime Minister Yatsanyuk and his colleagues are committed partners and understand that the Ukrainian Government has difficult reform choices to make after inheriting an economic mess from Yanukovych. Ukraine's considerable economic potential has never been matched by its business environment or economic leadership and now is the time to begin to get its financial house in order and realize its promise.

Second, deterring further encroachment on Ukrainian territory and pressing for an end to Russia's occupation of Crimea. President Obama has led a broad international condemnation of Russia's intervention with strong unified statements from the G7 and NATO, as well as the EU, whose leaders are meeting today in an emergency summit. We are sending international observers from the OSCE to Crimea and eastern Ukraine to bear witness to what is happening and make clear that minorities are not at risk. This was never a credible claim by Russia nor a credible pretext for military intervention.

We are making clear that there are costs for what Russia has already done and working with our partners to make clear that the costs will increase significantly if intervention expands. Today, as you mentioned, Mr. Chairman, the President signed an Executive order authorizing sanctions, including asset freezes and travel bans on individuals and entities responsible for activities undermining democratic processes or institutions in Ukraine, threatening the peace, security, stability, sovereignty, or territorial integrity of Ukraine, contributing to the misappropriation of state assets of Ukraine, or that purport to exercise authority over any part of Ukraine without authorization from the Ukrainian Government in Kiev. This EO will be used in a flexible way to designate those most directly involved in destabilizing Ukraine.

The State Department today also put in place visa restrictions on a number of officials and individuals. We continue to look at every aspect of our relationship with Russia, from suspension of preparations for the Sochi G8 summit to pausing key elements in our bilateral dialogue.

Third, bolstering Ukraine's neighbors. We are moving immediately to reinforce our Washington Treaty commitments to our allies. As Secretary Hagel stressed yesterday, we are taking concrete steps to support NATO partners through intensified joint training with our aviation detachment in Poland and enhanced participation in NATO's air policing mission in the Baltics.

Fourth, Secretary Kerry is working intensively to deescalate the crisis in order to restore Ukraine's sovereignty while creating a diplomatic offramp. We support direct dialogue between Kiev and Moscow, facilitated by an international contact group. The President and Secretary Kerry have emphasized we do not seek confrontation with Russia. It is clearly in the interest of both Ukraine and Russia to have a healthy relationship, born of centuries of cultural, economic, and social ties. The will for that exists among Ukraine's new leaders, but it cannot happen if Russia continues down its current dangerous and irresponsible path. That will only bring greater isolation and mounting costs for Russia.

Our strategy, it seems to me, needs to be steady and determined, mindful of what is at stake for Ukrainians as well as for international norms. We also need to be mindful of the enduring strengths of the United States and its partners and the very real weaknesses sometimes obscured by Russian bluster. Most of all, President Putin underestimates the commitment of Ukrainians across their country to sovereignty and independence and to writing their own future.

No one should underestimate the power of patient and resolute counterpressure using all of the nonmilitary means at our disposal, working with our allies, and leaving the door open to deescalation and diplomacy if Russia is prepared to play by international rules.

Now let me turn very briefly to the Levant. The turbulence of the past 3 years has had many roots: rising aspirations for dignity, political participation, and economic opportunity in a region in which too many people, for too many years, have been denied them, the ruthless reaction of some regimes and the efforts of violent extremists to exploit the resulting chaos. Nowhere have these trends converged more dangerously than in Syria. The conflict and the Assad regime have become a magnet for foreign fighters, many affiliated with terrorist groups from across the region and around the world.

As Matt will describe, these fighters, mostly Sunni extremists, represent a long-term threat to U.S. national security interests. From the other side, Assad has recruited thousands of foreign fighters, mostly Shia, to defend the regime, with active Iranian support and facilitation. The hard reality is that the grinding Syrian civil war is now an incubator of extremism on both sides of the sectarian divide.

We face a number of serious risks to our interests as a result: the risk to the homeland from global jihadist groups who seek to gain long-term safe havens, the risk to the stability of our regional partners, including Jordan, Lebanon, and Iraq, the risk to Israel and other partners from the rise of Iranian-backed extremist groups, especially Lebanese Hezbollah, fighting in Syria, and the risk to the Syrian people, whose suffering constitutes the greatest humanitarian crisis of this new century.

These are enormous challenges. They require a steady, comprehensive American strategy aimed at isolating extremists and bolstering moderates both inside Syria and amongst our regional partners. I would highlight briefly four elements of our strategy.

First, we are working to isolate and degrade terrorist networks in Syria. That means stepping up efforts with other governments to stem the flow of foreign fighters into Syria and cutting off financing and weapons to terrorist groups. It also means stepping up efforts to strengthen the moderate opposition, without which progress toward a negotiated transition of leadership through the Geneva process or any other diplomatic effort is impossible. Strengthened moderate forces are critical both to accelerate the demise of the Assad regime and to help Syrians build a counterweight to the extremists who threaten both the present and the post-Assad future of Syria and the region. None of this is easy, but the stakes are very high.

Second, we are pushing hard against Iranian financing and material support to its proxy groups in Syria and elsewhere. We are also working intensively with partners in the gulf and elsewhere to curb financing flows to extremists.

Third, we are increasing cooperation with Turkey and intensifying our efforts to strengthen the capacity of Syria's other endangered neighbors. In Jordan, which I visited again last month, we are further enhancing the capacity of the Jordanian Armed Forces to police its borders and deepening intelligence cooperation on extremist threats. The staggering burden of supporting 600,000 Syrian refugees has put serious strain on Jordan's resources. We deeply appreciate Congress' continued support for significant United States assistance for Jordan, which has totaled about a billion dollars for each of the past couple years, complemented by substantial loan guarantees. I can think of no better investment in regional stability than our efforts in Jordan.

In Lebanon, we are supporting the Lebanese Armed Forces to help deter spillover, better monitor the border with Syria, and help bolster the government's policy of disassociation from the Syrian conflict. The formation of a new Cabinet last month provides a renewed opportunity for the United States to engage, and Secretary Kerry reaffirmed our strong commitment to Lebanon's security and economic stability directly to President Sleiman and to the international support group for Lebanon ministerial meeting in Paris yesterday.

In Iraq, we are surging security assistance and information-sharing to combat the rising threat from ISIL, while pressing Iraqi leaders to execute a comprehensive strategy, security, policy, and economic, to isolate extremists, especially in Anbar. That was one of the main purposes of my last visit to Baghdad at the end of January.

I appreciate the close consultation we have had with you, Mr. Chairman, and with other members of the committee on these crucial issues.

Finally, we are supporting global efforts to ease the humanitarian crisis in Syria through the $1.7 billion we have already contributed.

Beyond the Levant, we continue to work with our gulf partners to enhance security cooperation, blunt the extremist threat, and support sound economic development in transitioning countries. This will be an important focus of the President's visit to Saudi Arabia later this month.

Mr. Chairman, the rise of extremism in the Levant poses an acute risk for the United States and for our regional partners. It is essential that we intensify our efforts to isolate extremists in Syria, limit the flow of foreign fighters, bolster moderate opposition forces, ease the humanitarian crisis, and help key partners like Jordan defend against spillover.

Thank you again for your focus on these vitally important issues and we look forward to continuing to work with you.

[The prepared statement of Ambassador Burns follows:]

PREPARED STATEMENT OF AMBASSADOR WILLIAM J. BURNS

Chairman Menendez, Ranking Member Corker, members of the committee, thank you for inviting me to address the challenges of growing extremism in the Levant.

My statement will discuss the nature of the extremist challenge in the Levant, the important interests at stake for the United States, and how we intend to advance and protect those interests over the coming months.

THE NATURE OF THE CHALLENGE

Over the past decade, aspirations for a better life have risen among populations across the Middle East. Sixty percent of the people in the region are under 30 years of age, and their ambitions—for economic opportunity, political expression, and basic human rights—ultimately burst onto the streets, from Tunisia, to Egypt, to Libya and Yemen, Bahrain and finally to Syria. Fueled by new technologies that enabled greater connectivity and individual political expression, populations across the region, often for the first time, sought to hold their leaders accountable.

There have been some successes, most notably in Tunisia, where a new pluralistic political system has begun to emerge, anchored by a just-ratified constitution, and in Yemen, where the first phase of a historic level of national consultation over the direction of the country has just been completed. But the broader trend is one of turbulent transformation, often exacerbated by regional rivalries and destabilizing interventions, including Iran's role in Syria. The initial exhilaration among those pressing for change has given way to the hard realization that lasting social and political transformation requires arduous effort, compromise, and time.

The rapid changes in the region have created vacuums and reopened long-dormant divisions within societies and along class, sectarian, and ethnic fault lines. Sectarian conflicts have reemerged, and the same technologies that facilitated peaceful popular movements have also been used to deepen societal fissures—spreading messages of hate and incitement against entire groups based solely on identity or affiliation.

Nowhere have these trends converged more powerfully than in Syria. There, 3 years ago, an authoritarian regime met peaceful protests with violent suppression and carnage. The fateful decision by the Assad regime to reject a meaningful political dialogue and violently suppress popular aspirations led to open, armed conflict. That conflict exacerbated existing ethnic, sectarian, and broader regional political tensions, fueling the extremism that is the topic of this hearing.

Among the many consequences of the Syria conflict, one of the most serious is the rise of extremism in the Levant. The conflict is now attracting foreign fighters from across the region and around the world. Many of these fighters are affiliated with designated terrorist groups, such as the al-Qaeda affiliated al-Nusra Front, and the formerly Iraq-based al-Qaeda affiliate now known as the Islamic State of Iraq and the Levant (ISIL). Both of these terrorist groups have sought to hijack the same popular aspirations the regime violently repressed.

As my colleague from the National Counterterrorism Center (NCTC) will discuss in more detail, NCTC now assesses there are nearly 23,000 extremist fighters in Syria, including more than 7,000 foreign fighters from as many as 50 countries. These fighters, mostly Sunni extremists, could represent a long-term threat to U.S. national security interests. Nusra and ISIL, have exploited largely ungoverned spaces in northern and eastern Syria to carve out territory to train fighters, recruit more of them, and plan attacks. Both groups have recently taken credit for terrorist operations in Lebanon, including one on the Lebanese Armed Forces. ISIL has also established camps in western Iraq and claimed terrorist operations in Iraq.

From the other side, thousands of foreign fighters (mostly Shia) have traveled to Syria to defend the Assad regime with active support from Iran and Lebanese Hezbollah in recruiting and fighting. We believe the majority of these fighters come from Lebanon and Iraq. They are recruited on the premise of defending holy sites in Syria, but have been observed in battle across Syria. The foreign fighters' presence exacerbates the conflict's sectarian dimension and has led to lethal competition with the indigenous Syrian opposition.

The grinding Syrian conflict is now an incubator of extremism—on both sides of the sectarian divide. Controversial Sunni clerics have called on able-bodied Sunni men to travel to Syria to fight in a foreign war against what they brand a Shia regime. Radical Shia clerics such as Hassan Nasrallah, the head of the high profile Shia extremist group Hezbollah in Lebanon, have called on able-bodied Shiites to fight those they brand ''Takfiris'' fighting on the side of the opposition.

It is important to note that the conflict in Syria is not primarily a clash between the Shia and Sunni branches of Islam, but rather a clash between a small minority of violent extremists against the vast majority of moderates, whether Sunni or Shia, who seek to realize the promise of economic and political modernization. The extremists fueling the flames of conflict are outliers. To put that in perspective, while there may be up to 23,000 fighters among the rebel ranks inside Syria, the total number of opposition fighters is estimated between 75,000 and 110,000.

Despite the sectarian dimension of the Syria conflict, we also believe that it is a mistake to describe it as simply a proxy war between Iran and Saudi Arabia. To do so obscures the origins of the Syria conflict, which began as a nonviolent movement for political change. And it trivializes the sacrifice of the many Syrian men and women who do not identify with extremists from the Sunni or Shia camps, and who have stood up to an oppressive regime for basic political rights. It would be a mistake to dismiss this moderate majority, who stand against violent extremist groups on both sides of the conflict. The United States has no interest in taking sides in a contest between Sunni and Shia, whether in Syria, Lebanon, Iraq, or anywhere else in the region. Instead, as President Obama has stated: ''What we are trying to do is take sides against extremists of all sorts and in favor of people who are in favor of moderation, tolerance, representative government, and over the long term, stability and prosperity for the people of Syria.''

That statement encapsulates our fundamental objective, not only in Syria—but also throughout the Levant and the broader region.

U.S. INTERESTS AT STAKE

There are four immediate risks to U.S. interests from the Syrian conflict and the rise of extremist groups in the Levant.

First, there is the risk of external operations by al-Qaeda affiliated or inspired groups, such as al-Nusra and ISIL. We know that some of these groups seek long-term safe haven from which to expand their base of operations for attacks throughout the region and potentially the West.

Second, there is the risk to the stability of our partners in the region, including Lebanon, Jordan, and Iraq. In Lebanon, there are now nearly 1 million refugees from Syria, roughly 20 percent of the population prior to the Syrian conflict, and sectarian tensions are spilling over the Syria-Lebanon border. Lebanon has experienced car bombs in Beirut and elsewhere and gunfights in the flashpoint city of Tripoli. Shia-populated border towns have been the target of direct attacks by ISIL, Nusra, and its allies in the Islamic Front, and Sunni towns by the Assad regime. In Jordan, nearly 600,000 Syrian refugees, more than 10 percent of the population, are stressing limited resources. Despite an unprecedented international humanitarian response, both Jordanian and Lebanese governments are struggling to deal with the strain. In Iraq, the two-way flow of extremist fighters—and the rise of ISIL—has increased violent attacks to levels not seen since 2007, with nearly 1,000 Iraqis killed in January 2014 alone.

Third, there is the risk to Israel and Arab partners in the region from the rise of Iranian-backed extremist groups, especially Lebanese Hezbollah, as well as the dangers when battle-seasoned Sunni fighters return to their home countries. In the case of Yemen, we see young men from both sides of the sectarian divide going to the fight, with plans to return to Yemen to use those skills. Fighters from the Iranian-backed groups are now gaining battlefield experience through regular rotations to Syria and advanced military training, including at training camps in Iran.

Fourth, there is the risk to the Syrian people, whose suffering constitutes the greatest humanitarian crisis the world has seen in this new century. Approximately 9.3 million people inside Syria are in need of humanitarian assistance, and well over 100,000 have now been killed since the conflict began. As in all conflicts, the suffering of the most vulnerable population elements is the greatest. Polio has returned to eastern Syria, where conflict disrupted vaccination programs. And we are increasingly concerned about a potential "lost generation" of Syrian children now living as refugees or internally displaced persons, many of whom are traumatized and without access to education, medicine or adequate food.

U.S. STRATEGY: BOLSTER MODERATES, ISOLATE EXTREMISTS, SHORE UP NEIGHBORS

To mitigate these risks and protect U.S. interests, our strategy must focus both on immediate and long-term initiatives that leverage existing security relationships with key partners. In the long-term, as explained by the President, we face a struggle—not between Sunni and Shia, or Iran and Saudi Arabia—but between extremists and moderates. Our policy is to isolate extremists and bolster moderates—a critical mass of the population—both in Syria and in the greater region. Over the long term, this requires a steady focus on supporting economic and political modernization. In the immediate term, we are focused on mitigating risks stemming from the Syria conflict and the rise of extremism and extremist groups in the Levant, and on shoring up Syria's neighbors. We will work along four lines of effort, focused on the most acute risks to U.S. national security interests.

First, we will work to isolate and degrade terrorist networks in Syria. As my NCTC colleague will address in detail, it is essential that we work with regional and international partners to police and stem the flow of foreign fighters into and out of Syria on both sides of the conflict. For example, we are working with Turkey on border security, and we have robust security cooperation with Jordan. We are encouraged by laws recently enacted by Saudi Arabia, which made it illegal for Saudis to fight in a foreign conflict, a topic that the President will discuss with King Abdullah of Saudi Arabia later this month in Riyadh. We are also pressing regional partners to stop the flow of finances and weapons to terrorist groups, including designated terrorist groups like Nusra and ISIL. Our partners are concerned about the lure of the battlefield to their young men, and the potential for violent extremism blowback in their own countries. We are encouraging them to look at a range of tools to discourage flows of money and fighters to the battlefield.

In parallel, we are working to further enhance the capacity of the moderate Syrian opposition, both inside and outside Syria. It is important to bear in mind that moderate insurgent groups now face a two-front war—against the Assad regime on one side, and ISIL on the other side. The moderate groups are an ally against ISIL, a point its leaders repeatedly made during the international talks held recently in Montreux and Geneva. The willingness of the moderate insurgents to confront ISIL is an important development. The Assad regime itself, heavily dependent on the "shabiha" militias and the assistance of Hezbollah and Iran, is most responsible for introducing terrorists to the Syrian conflict.

The success of our efforts to isolate and defeat violent extremist networks in Syria—their leadership, weapons, and financing—depends on negotiating a transition to a new leadership, without illusion about how long and difficult this process is likely to be. The United States will continue to work closely with the U.N., Russia, and the London 11 to support the Geneva process and press the regime to accept the key elements of the June 2012 Geneva communique, including a Transitional Governing Body. However imperfect, the Geneva process, when combined with other measures, represents the best chance we have to negotiate an end to this bloody conflict. And we will consider additional diplomatic means by which to bring this about.

Second, we will work to strengthen the capacity of Syria's neighbors, particularly Jordan, Lebanon, and Iraq. As we work to isolate and degrade the violent extremist networks in Syria, we must work in parallel to enhance the capacity of Syria's neighbors to mitigate the spillover effects of the conflict. Over the past 6 months, I have visited neighboring capitals to help coordinate our efforts. This included a visit in late January to Amman and then Baghdad, where I met with senior officials, including King Abdullah and Prime Minister Maliki, to discuss the Syria situation. Our relationships with these countries are multifaceted, but the key points include:

In Jordan, we have heard King Abdullah's concerns about the risks of extremist spillover from Syria. We are increasing assistance to the Jordanian Armed Forces (JAF) to police its sensitive borders and guard against external threats, and are sharing information about the violent extremist threats emanating from Syria.

CENTCOM Commander General Austin has also been consulting closely with his Jordanian counterparts. To support Jordan, we have provided $300 million per year in military assistance to the JAF and $360 million per year in economic support to address long-term development. We look forward to continuing this strong relationship in support of Jordan's economic and security reforms. We are also committed to supporting Jordan as it contends with the staggering costs of hosting nearly 600,000 Syrian refugees. To that end, we have provided cash transfers totaling $300 million in the last 2 fiscal years; supported a $1.25 billion U.S.-backed loan guarantee; and provided more than $268 million toward the humanitarian needs of Syrian refugees in Jordan. We appreciate congressional support for these additional needs and will continue to provide assistance to help Jordan address challenges arising from the Syrian crisis. As you know, King Abdullah was in the United States last month to discuss these and other initiatives with President Obama, Secretary Kerry, Secretary Hagel, other Cabinet Members and the Congress. Jordan is a cornerstone of regional stability and King Abdullah, one of our closest partners in the region, heard a staunch message of U.S. support to help protect Jordan against violent extremist threats and maintain support for the Jordanian economy.

In Lebanon, we are supporting the Lebanese Armed Forces (LAF) and the Internal Security Forces to deter violent extremist spillover from Syria. Since 2005, the United States has allocated nearly $1 billion to support the LAF and Internal Security Forces, and we are engaged with the Saudi Arabian Government to so that its recent pledge of $3 billion is used in a manner that complements our mutual goal to build up LAF capabilities. The U.S. commitment to a strong, independent, and sovereign Lebanon is steadfast, particularly as the country faces political challenges and spillover effects from Syria. During my last visit to Beirut, I met with senior political officials and military commanders, including President Sleiman and the LAF Commander, General Kahwagi. The impact from the Syrian conflict was central in all of my conversations, particularly as the LAF had just suffered casualties during an engagement with violent extremists in Sidon, a majority Sunni town south of Beirut. The refugee crisis has affected more than 1,600 communities across Lebanon. Secretary Kerry participated in the March 5 International Support Group for Lebanon ministerial in Paris to demonstrate our ongoing partnership with the Lebanese people, our support for development of the Lebanese Armed Forces, and our intention of working with the new Cabinet to help Lebanon address its security and economic challenges. The United States will continue to reinforce the generous humanitarian response from the Lebanese Government, including with the $76 million that we have contributed in humanitarian assistance to support refugees and host communities in Lebanon just this year, part of the $340 million we have contributed to the humanitarian effort in Lebanon since 2011. Politically, we strongly support efforts to ensure that upcoming elections are conducted in a timely, transparent, and fair manner in keeping with Lebanon's Constitution. Lebanon's leaders must meet their international obligations; all parties must adhere to the official policy of ''dissociation'' from the Syrian conflict.

In Iraq, we are prioritizing security assistance to combat the rising threat from ISIL, while pressing Iraqi leaders to execute a holistic strategy comprising security, political, and economic elements to isolate extremists over the long-term. During my recent visit to Baghdad, I discussed with leaders from all political blocs the need to pull together to address the ISIL threat. My conversations focused in particular on the situation in Ramadi and Fallujah, where ISIL has attempted to assert control and install local governance structures. The threat from ISIL is real, with materiel and suicide bombers flowing between Iraq and Syria, and executing a coordinated campaign meant to overthrow the Shia-led government, in part by conducting widespread indiscriminate attacks against Sunnis, Shia, and Kurds, and other populations in Iraq. We are encouraged by the response in Ramadi, where the central government is working in coordination with local leaders and tribes to expel violent extremist fighters from populated areas. The central government has approved approximately $128 million in assistance to meet humanitarian and reconstruction needs as well as support for tribes fighting ISIL. The Government of Iraq has also established a National Crisis Cell to coordinate assistance to Iraqis displaced by the recent sectarian violence in Anbar. We are now working with the Iraqis to help ensure that this money is allocated as rapidly as possible. Thanks to close cooperation from this committee and the Congress, we also bolstering the Iraqi Security Forces (ISF) with equipment needed in the counterterrorism fight, including Hellfire missiles. These missiles have proven effective at seriously damaging ISIL training camps in western Iraq, and we will continue to work closely with the ISF to ensure that they are employed with precision and on the basis of sound intelligence. The future delivery of six Apache helicopters, thanks again to support from this committee, will further improve the ISF's ability to target ISIL safe havens in western

Iraq. We will work to ensure that Iraq strictly complies with its end-use obligations for these helicopters. We will also work to ensure that Iraq resists negative pressure from Iran, including accepting offers from Iran for security assistance, which would be a clear violation of international sanctions. Finally, we are pressing to ensure that Iraq's national elections, scheduled for April 30, are held on time. Elections and inclusive politics remain essential for isolating violent extremists.

Third, we are pushing hard against Iranian financing and material support to its proxy groups in Syria and elsewhere. As we work closely with our gulf partners to enhance security cooperation, blunt the violent extremist threat, and support sound economic development, we are also continuing our close partnerships to identify and disrupt Iranian support to its proxy groups. We have assisted the governments in the region and around the world in investigating Iranian and Lebanese Hezbollah-directed terrorist attacks and plots. Our diplomatic efforts resulted in the Gulf Cooperation Council announcing their intent to blacklist Hezbollah, and the EU's designation in 2013 of Hezbollah's military wing as a terrorist organization. In parallel, we are continuing aggressive and ongoing enforcement of counterterrorism sanctions against Iran, including a series of designations last month by the Department of the Treasury. Over the past few years we have also identified the Lebanese Canadian Bank and two Lebanese exchange houses as foreign financial institutions of "primary money laundering concern," under Section 311 of the USA PATRIOT Act due to provision of support to Lebanese Hezbollah.

We are also working with our gulf partners to detect and interdict shipments of Iranian weaponry to proxies in the region. We have repeatedly intercepted Iranian shipments of weapons to militants in Yemen, Afghanistan, and Gaza. Earlier this year, Bahraini authorities seized a boat filled with Iranian explosives and arrested a dozen militants meant to receive the smuggled cargo. We are also continuing to press the Government of Iraq to enhance its inspection of flights traveling from Iran to Syria via Iraqi airspace. While the government has taken some action in this regard, it has not been enough—a message I pressed directly with Prime Minister Maliki and other key leaders during my recent visit to Baghdad.

Fourth, we support global efforts to address the humanitarian crisis in Syria. Violent extremist groups thrive in atmospheres of popular grievance, human suffering, and the collapse of state authority. Beyond the humanitarian and moral imperative, there are hard-nosed security dimensions to our global effort to address the human costs of the conflict inside Syria. The Syrian conflict represents this young century's greatest humanitarian crisis, with the largest refugee outflows in recent history. As we undertake negotiations with Israelis and Palestinians, in which refugee right of return is among the most contentious issues, it is not hard to see the potential for the humanitarian aspect of Syria's conflict to further disrupt the Middle East region for decades to come. The United States is the largest international donor of humanitarian assistance to the Syrian people. At the recent donor conference in Kuwait, Secretary Kerry pledged an additional $380 million in humanitarian assistance, bringing our total assistance to date to more than $1.7 billion. We also continue to press through the Geneva process and the U.N. Security Council to expand humanitarian access to Syrians. The recent adoption of a U.N. Security Council resolution demanding safe and unhindered humanitarian access to civilians in Syria was an important step in that effort and we will press for its full implementation.

CONCLUSION

The reasons for the rise of extremism in the Levant are complicated and flow in part from the profound changes that have swept the region in the past 3 years. The conflict in Syria and the wave of foreign fighters it has attracted from both sides of the sectarian divide have exacerbated extremism and sectarianism in the Levant, and represent an acute risk to U.S. interests.

We are under no illusions that the framework I have articulated will immediately blunt violent extremism in the Levant, but a strategy to isolate extremist groups, bolster opposition moderates, shore up Syria's neighbors and address the humanitarian crisis offers the best chance in the near term to mitigate these acute risks. We look forward to working closely with the Congress to address these challenges.

Thank you again for allowing me to address this important topic. I look forward to your questions.

The CHAIRMAN. Thank you, Mr. Secretary.

I would like to take in one more set of testimony, then recess briefly for the vote and immediately come back. So, Mr. Secretary.

STATEMENT OF HON. DEREK CHOLLET, ASSISTANT SECRETARY OF DEFENSE FOR INTERNATIONAL SECURITY AFFAIRS, U.S. DEPARTMENT OF DEFENSE, WASHINGTON, DC

Mr. CHOLLET. Thanks. Mr. Chairman, Senator Corker, members of the committee, I appreciate the opportunity to speak with you today about security threats in the Middle East and how our regional defense policy addresses these challenges, and I will keep my opening comments very brief.

As Deputy Secretary Burns described, sectarianism and extremism pose grave threats to the well-being and aspirations of the people of the Middle East, the stability and security of our regional partners, and U.S. national security interests. That is why our regional defense strategy is centered on cooperating with regional partners. The historic transformation in the region we have witnessed during the last 3 years offers the United States both opportunities and challenges as we work to address our core security interests, first, to combat al-Qaeda and associated movements; second, to confront external aggression directed at our allies; third, to ensure the free flow of energy from the region; and fourth, to prevent the development, proliferation, and use of weapons of mass destruction.

As U.S. military forces have withdrawn from Iraq and now Afghanistan, we are also addressing questions from our regional partners about our intentions in the region and our commitments over the long term. We are working hard to sustain and enhance our military capabilities in the region.

As Secretary Hagel said in his speech in Manama last December, the United States has enduring security interests in the region and we remain fully committed to the security of our allies and our regional partners. We have a military presence of more than 35,000 personnel in and immediately around the Arabian Gulf, and the Quadrennial Defense Review that the Department released several days ago reaffirms this commitment, and, despite budget pressures, we will maintain a robust force posture in the region.

I would like to briefly touch on some examples of how we are working to improve the military capabilities of our partners, focusing on Iraq, Lebanon, and Jordan. First, in Iraq, along with our State Department colleagues, we have been advising the Iraqi Government that the long-term strategy to defeat ISIL and achieving stability and security must include a political solution involving all the people of Iraq. And while the Iraqi security forces have proven competent at conducting counterterrorism and stability operations, the security situation they face there is very serious.

The Iraqis also have gaps in their ability to defend against external threats and in areas such as integrated air defense, intelligence-sharing, and logistics. We remain very committed to working with the Iraqi Government to develop its military and security abilities. As this committee knows very well, the Iraqis are also asking to acquire key capabilities from the United States as soon as possible. We appreciate the quick decision to proceed with the Hellfire missiles notification associated with this urgent request. The Iraqis have paid about $250 million toward the resupply and we have been able to expedite the delivery of tank rounds, rockets, small arms, and ammunition. Those articles have either been delivered or are expected to arrive in the next few weeks. Associated with that request, we deeply appreciate your support to move forward with the sale and the lease of Apache helicopters.

Turning to Lebanon, we view the Lebanese Armed Forces' emergence as the sole legitimate defense force as a critical component of Lebanon's long-term stability and development. U.S. assistance to the Lebanese Armed Forces and internal security forces, which is approximately $1 billion in assistance since 2005, strengthens Lebanese capacity and supports its mission to secure its own borders. We work to maintain strong ties between Lebanese and U.S. officers and officials through IMET, and Lebanon has the fourth-largest IMET program in the world. We are also promoting institutional reform through a Defense Institution Reform Initiative, or DIRI, with the LAF and efforts supporting Lebanese security sector reform.

In Jordan, we are deeply committed to maintaining a strong defense partnership. Today and tomorrow, I am hosting the Jordanian Chief of Defense, General Zabban, at the Pentagon and his entire team for a series of meetings. As Deputy Burns said, we have no better defense partner than Jordan.

U.S. security assistance helps build the capacity of the Jordanian Armed Forces, promotes interoperability between our two militaries, enhances Jordan's border security and counterterrorism capabilities, and supports military education and training. We provide the Jordanian Government with approximately $300 million in FMF funds per year. We have an active joint exercise program along with a very robust officer exchange program.

In response to the crisis in Syria, we have military forces in Jordan manning a Patriot battery, an F–16 unit, and assisting the Jordanians with the planning necessary to strengthen its defense. In addition, we are providing equipment and training that will supplement the Jordanians' border security program and improve the capability of the Jordanian military to detect and interdict illegal attempts to cross the border and detect attempts to smuggle WMD along the border.

Mr. Chairman, members of the committee, through these efforts in Iraq, Lebanon, Jordan, and elsewhere, the Department of Defense is keenly focused on building the capacity of our partners to fight extremism and support U.S. national security interests, and we remain committed to continuing to work with this committee and the Congress on these critical issues. I look forward to your questions.

[The prepared statement of Mr. Chollet follows:]

PREPARED STATEMENT OF ASSISTANT SECRETARY DEREK CHOLLET

Chairman Menendez, Senator Corker, members of the committee, I appreciate the opportunity to speak to you today about extremism and sectarianism in the Middle East, and how our regional defense policy addresses these challenges.

As Deputy Secretary Burns and Director Olson described, sectarianism and extremism pose grave threats to the well-being and aspirations of the people of the Middle East, the stability and security of our regional partners, and U.S. national security interests.

That's why our regional defense strategy is centered on cooperating with regional partners to achieve a stable, peaceful, and prosperous Middle East, one which promotes democracy, human rights, and open markets. The historic transformation in the region we've witnessed during the last 3 years offers the United States both opportunities and challenges as we work to address our core security interests: to combat al-Qaeda and associated movements; to confront external aggression directed at our allies; to ensure the free flow of energy from the region; and to prevent the development, proliferation, and use of weapons of mass destruction (WMD).

As U.S. military forces have withdrawn from Iraq and now Afghanistan, we are also addressing questions from our regional partners about our intentions in the region, and our commitments to our long-term allies. We are working hard to sustain and enhance our military capabilities in the region.

As Secretary Hagel reassured our regional partners in a speech in Manama last December, the United States has enduring military interests in this region, and we will remain fully committed to the security of our allies and our regional partners. We have a presence of more than 35,000 military personnel in and immediately around the gulf. The U.S. Army continues to maintain more than 10,000 forward-deployed soldiers; we have deployed advanced fighter aircraft, including F–22s; we have advanced intelligence, surveillance and reconnaissance assets; we have fielded ballistic missile defense ships and PATRIOT batteries; and we maintain over 40 ships in the region. Our commitment to our core interests is absolute.

I would like to briefly touch on some examples on how we are working to improve the military capabilities of our partners—focusing on Iraq, Lebanon, and Jordan.

In Iraq, we are deeply concerned by the Islamic State in Iraq and the Levant's (ISIL) growing reach and lethality. Along with our State Department colleagues, we have been advising the Iraqi Government that the long-term strategy to defeat ISIL and achieving security and stability must include a political solution involving all of the people of Iraq.

While the Iraqi Security Forces have proven competent at conducting counterterrorism and stability operations, the security situation they face is very serious. The Iraqis also have gaps in their ability to defend against external threats and in areas such as integrated air defense, intelligence-sharing, and logistics. We remain very committed to working with the Iraqi Government to develop its military and security abilities.

As this committee knows, the Iraqis are also asking for increased Foreign Military Sales of key capabilities as soon as possible. We appreciate the quick decision to proceed with the Hellfire missiles notification associated with the urgent request. The Iraqis have paid about $250 million toward the resupply, and we have been able to expedite the delivery of tank rounds, rocket, small arms and ammunition. Those articles have either been delivered or are expected to arrive in the next few weeks.

Associated with that request, we deeply appreciate your support to move forward the sale and lease of the Apache helicopters.

Turning to Lebanon: We remain deeply concerned with Iran's destabilizing activities in Lebanon and its partnership with Hezbollah. We view the Lebanese Armed Forces' emergence as the sole legitimate defense force as a critical component of Lebanon's long-term stability and development. U.S. assistance to Lebanese Armed Forces (LAF) and Internal Security Forces, approximately $1 billion in assistance since 2005, strengthens the capacity of the Lebanese Armed Forces and supports its mission to secure Lebanon's borders, defend the sovereignty of the state, and implement U.N. Security Council Resolutions 1559 and 1701.

Lebanon's International Military Education and Training (IMET) program is the fourth-largest in the world. IMET builds strong ties between the United States and Lebanon by bringing Lebanese officers and officials to the United States to study and train alongside U.S. troops.

In terms of supporting institutional reform, the Department of Defense has just started a Defense Institution Reform Initiative (DIRI) with the LAF. DIRI complements a U.S. whole-of-government effort supporting Lebanese security sector reform. U.S. Central Command (USCENTCOM) continues to provide support to the training and professionalization of the LAF while the Department of State's Bureau of International Narcotics and Law Enforcement Affairs (INL) is funding a program to strengthen the capability and management capacity of the Internal Security Forces (ISF).

In Jordan, we are deeply committed to maintaining a strong defense partnership. And today and tomorrow, I am hosting the Jordanian Chief of Defense and his senior team for intensive meetings at the Pentagon. U.S. security assistance helps build the capacity of the Jordanian Armed Forces; promotes interoperability between our two militaries; enhances Jordan's border security and counterterrorism capabilities; and supports military education and training.

We have provided the Jordanian Government with approximately $300 million in FMF funds per year. An active joint exercise program, along with a robust exchange officer program, cements our military relationship.

We have military forces in Jordan manning a Patriot battery and F–16 unit, and assisting the Jordanians with the planning necessary to strengthen its defense.

In addition, we are providing equipment and training that will supplement the Jordan Border Security Program and improve the capability of the Jordanian military to detect and interdict illegal attempts to cross the border, and detect attempts to smuggle WMD along the border.

Mr. Chairman, members of this committee, through these efforts in Iraq, Lebanon, Jordan, and elsewhere, the Department of Defense is keenly focused on building the capacity of our partners to fight extremism and support U.S. national security interests. And we remain committed to continuing to work with this committee and the Congress on these critical issues.

The CHAIRMAN. Thank you, Mr. Secretary.

What we are going to do is I am going to have the committee go into recess, cast one vote. The Chair will come immediately back. Those who are interested I would urge to come back as well. We will hear from Director Olsen and then we will proceed to questions.

The committee will be in recess subject to the call of the Chair.

[Recess from 11:35 a.m. to 11:48 a.m.]

The CHAIRMAN. The hearing will come back to order, with thanks and our apologies to our witnesses. You will be happy to know, Mr. Secretary, that Ms. Gottemoeller was confirmed.

Director Olsen.

STATEMENT OF HON. MATTHEW G. OLSEN, DIRECTOR, NATIONAL COUNTERTERRORISM CENTER, WASHINGTON, DC

Mr. OLSEN. Thank you very much, Mr. Chairman and members of the committee.

I think it was about a year ago I was here to talk about threats in North Africa, so I appreciate the opportunity to be here again to represent NCTC and to talk a little bit about the threats we face in the Levant. I am particularly pleased to be here with two of our key partners, Deputy Secretary of State Burns and Assistant Secretary of Defense Chollet.

As you are aware, we continue to face terrorist threats to the United States and to our interests overseas, particularly in parts of South Asia and the Middle East and Africa. But it is the current conflict in Syria and the regional instability in the Levant that stand out for me as areas of particular concern. I do think it is important to consider Syria in the context of the global terrorist movement. In the face of what has been sustained counterterrorism pressure, core al-Qaeda has adapted. They have adapted by becoming more decentralized and shifting away from the large-scale plotting that was exemplified in the attacks of September 11.

Al-Qaeda has modified its tactics and look to conduct simpler attacks that do not require the same degree of resources and training and command and control. So today we are facing a wider array of threats in a greater variety of locations across the Middle East and around the world. In comparison to the al-Qaeda plots that emanated from the tribal areas of Pakistan a few years ago, these smaller and these less sophisticated plots are often more difficult for us to detect and disrupt, and that puts even greater pressure on us to work closely with our partners here at the table, across the Federal Government, and around the world.

Turning to Syria, Syria has become the preeminent location for al-Qaeda-aligned groups to recruit and to train and to equip what is now a growing number of extremists, some of whom seek to conduct external attacks. In addition, Iran and Hezbollah, as you pointed out, are committed to defending the Assad regime, including sending billions of dollars in military and economic aid, training pro-regime and Iraqi Shia militants, and deploying their own personnel into the country.

Now, from a terrorism perspective, the most concerning development is that al-Qaeda has declared Syria its most critical front and has called for extremists to fight against the regime in Syria. So what we have seen is that thousands of fighters from around the world, including hundreds from the West, have traveled to Syria and many of them have joined with established terrorist groups in Syria. This raises our concern that radicalized individuals with extremist contacts and battlefield experience could return to their home countries to commit violence at their own initiative or participate in al-Qaeda-directed plots aimed at Western targets outside of Syria.

What we have seen is a coalescence in Syria of al-Qaeda veterans from Afghanistan and Pakistan, as well as extremists from other hot spots such as Libya and Iraq. These extremists bring a wide range of contacts and skills, as well as battlefield experience, and they are able to exploit what has become a permissive environment from which to plot and train.

Shifting briefly to Lebanon, one of the continuing effects of the Syrian conflict will be the instability in Lebanon in the upcoming year. I recently traveled to Lebanon and Jordan and the impacts of the continuing conflict in Syria continue to be of great concern to officials in the region.

Hezbollah publicly admitted last spring that it is fighting for the Syrian regime and has framed the war as an act of self-defense against Western-backed Sunni extremists. The group is sending capable fighters for pro-regime operations and support for pro-regime militias. In addition, Iran and Hezbollah are using allied Iraqi Shia groups to participate in counteropposition operations. This active support to the Assad regime is, of course, driving increased Sunni extremist attacks and sectarian violence.

In short, the various factors contributing to instability in Lebanon are only exacerbated by the protracted conflict in Syria.

Finally, I will turn to Iraq. What we have witnessed there over the last 3 years is a resurgence by the Islamic State for Iraq and the Levant, or ISIL, the former group known as AQI. The group has a core cadre of veteran extremists and access to a steady flow of weapons and fighters from Syria. So last year ISIL suicide and car bomb attacks returned to their peak levels from what we saw back in 2007 and 2008. At the end of last year the group was averaging one suicide attack per day.

The situation in Fallujah is particularly disconcerting, where hundreds of ISIL fighters have joined the ranks with former insurgent groups to consolidate control of the inner city and contest areas in neighboring towns.

In sum, the threat posed by ISIL to our interests in the region is growing, not diminishing. In the period ahead we will be working closely with our colleagues from State and Defense to aid the Iraqi Government's counterterrorism efforts.

The last point I will make is that, in light of the large foreign fighter component in the Syrian crisis, we are working together to gather every piece of information we can about the identities of these individuals. As you know, at NCTC we play a role in supporting the effort to watch-list individuals and our efforts support the broader aviation and border screening efforts of our partners at the FBI and the Department of Homeland Security, and we are engaged in a focused effort to track the travel of any of these individuals, particularly from the West to Syria. As the conflict in Syria continues, the issues associated with Syrian foreign fighters and their travel patterns will be a continued area of the highest priority for us at NCTC.

So in closing, Mr. Chairman, I want to assure you we are focused on the threat environment in this part of the world and we are working to identify and disrupt threats to the United States and particularly to our personnel serving in these areas. We will continue to support our whole of government effort in the region by identifying and analyzing threat-information, sharing that information with our partners across the government. On behalf of the men and women at NCTC, I want to thank you for inviting me here to testify and for your focus on these critical issues.

Thank you.

[The prepared statement of Mr. Olsen follows:]

PREPARED STATEMENT OF HON. MATTHEW G. OLSEN

INTRODUCTION

Thank you Chairman Menendez, Ranking Member Corker, and members of the committee. I appreciate this opportunity to be here today to represent the National Counterterrorism Center (NCTC) and discuss with you the threat of terrorism and extremism in Syria, Iraq, and Lebanon.

Intelligence Community leaders have testified over the past few weeks on the overall counterterrorism picture, noting that we face an enduring threat to U.S. interests overseas—particularly in parts of South Asia, the Middle East, and Africa. However, the regional instability in the Levant and increasingly in Iraq certainly stands out as an area of increasing concern.

The current stalemate in Syria is having a ripple effect in Iraq, in Lebanon, and throughout the region; this is of great concern to the United States, and impacts more than just our counterterrorism equities. There are important defense and geopolitical considerations as well. Therefore, I am particularly pleased to be here today with two of NCTC's key partners—Deputy Secretary of State Burns and Assistant Secretary of Defense Chollet.

THE CURRENT STATE OF AL-QAEDA

It is important to consider the current conflict and regional instability in Iraq and the Levant region in the context of the global terrorist movement. In the face of sustained counterterrorism pressure, core al-Qaeda has adapted by becoming more decentralized and is shifting away from large-scale, mass casualty plots like the attacks of September 11. Al-Qaeda has modified its tactics, looking to conduct simpler attacks that do not require the same degree of resources, training, and command and control.

Instability in the Middle East and North Africa has accelerated this decentralization of the al-Qaeda movement, which is increasingly influenced by local and regional factors and conditions. This diffusion has also led to the emergence of new power centers and an increase in threats by networks of like-minded violent extremists with allegiances to multiple groups. Ultimately, this less centralized network poses a more diverse and geographically dispersed threat and is likely to result in increased low-level attacks against U.S. and European interests overseas. Put simply, we are facing a wider array of threats in a greater variety of locations across the Middle East and around the world. In comparison to the al-Qaeda plots that emanated from the tribal areas of Pakistan a few years ago, these smaller, less sophisticated plots are often more difficult to detect and disrupt, putting even greater pressure on us to work closely with partners around the world.

Last year, counterterrorism operations and the loss of key al-Qaeda leaders and members further degraded al-Qaeda core's ability to lead the global terrorist movement and to plan sophisticated attacks in the West. While we continue to assess that al-Qaeda senior leaders remain the recognized leader of the global terrorist movement, their leadership and authority have not gone unchallenged, as the rift between core al-Qaeda and the Islamic State of Iraq and Levant (ISIL) makes abundantly clear. We are still assessing the full impact of the recent statement from Ayman al-Zawahiri publicly disassociating al-Qaeda from ISIL.

Returning now to current terrorist threats in Iraq and the across the Levant, these emanate from a diverse array of actors, ranging from formal groups—such as al-Qaeda and its affiliates, Lebanese Hezbollah, and the ISIL—to a large pool of individuals—many of them from Western countries including the United States—only loosely affiliated or attached to groups we are tracking.

This morning I will break down the terrorist threat from this region as we see it in the Intelligence Community. I'll start with Syria, then move to Lebanon and Iraq, and finally close with some of the activities we're engaged in to identify Syrian foreign fighters.

Syria

Syria has become the preeminent location for independent or al-Qaeda-aligned groups to recruit, train, and equip a growing number of extremists, some of whom we assess may seek to conduct external attacks. Hostilities between Sunni and Shia are also intensifying in Syria and spilling into neighboring countries—particularly Lebanon—which is increasing the likelihood of a protracted conflict in Syria as both seek military advantage.

Both the Syrian regime and the opposition believe that they can achieve a military victory in the ongoing conflict. President Assad remains unwilling to negotiate himself out of power—currently an untenable outcome for the opposition forces—and he almost certainly intends to remain the ruler of Syria and to win a new 7-year term in Presidential elections that might occur mid-year.

To that end, Iran and Hezbollah are committed to defending the Assad regime, including sending billions of dollars in military and economic aid, training pro-regime and Iraqi Shia militants, and deploying their own personnel into the country. Iran and Hezbollah view the Assad regime as a key partner in an "axis of resistance" against Israel and are prepared to take major risks to preserve the regime as well as their critical transshipment routes.

In terms of the opposition, the fight against the Assad Regime includes up to 110,000 insurgents, who are organized into numerous groups, including more than 7,000 foreign fighters from 50 countries. European governments estimate that more than 1,000 Westerners have traveled to join the fight against the Assad regime. Dozens of Americans from a variety of backgrounds and locations in the United States have traveled or attempted to travel to Syria but to date we have not identified an organized recruitment effort targeting Americans. The U.S. Government continues to work closely with our foreign partners to resolve the identities of potential extremists and identify potential threats emanating from Syria.

Al-Qaeda amir Ayman al-Zawahiri and other prominent Salafist leaders continue to issue statements declaring Syria the most critical front for ideologically driven terrorism today and calling for additional fighters to support the cause. Ousting Assad in Syria has become a top al-Qaeda priority, and some of the most militarily effective antiregime forces are also those most closely aligned with al-Qaeda's violent extremist ideology.

At present, several extremist groups, including the al-Qaeda-linked al-Nusra Front and ISIL are in Syria fighting against the Assad regime. ISIL founded al-Nusra Front in late 2011 to act as its operational arm in Syria, although the two groups split following a public dispute in April 2013. Al-Nusra Front has mounted suicide, explosive, and firearms attacks against regime and security targets across the country; it has also sought to provide limited public services and governance to the local population in areas under its control.

Al-Nusra Front's leader, Abu Muhammad al-Jawlani, in April 2013 pledged allegiance to al-Qaeda leader Ayman al-Zawahiri, publicly affirming the group's ties to core al-Qaeda, and al-Zawahiri named the group al-Qaeda's recognized affiliate later last year. Many moderate opposition groups fight alongside al-Nusra Front and other Sunni extremists in Syria and depend on extremists for resources, including weapons and training.

Syria has already become a significant location for extremist groups to recruit, train, and equip a growing number of fighters. The combination of ungoverned areas as new safe havens, the presence inside Syria of experienced al-Qaeda terrorists and other seasoned extremists, and the influx of Westerners and other foreign fighters creates a fertile environment for external attack planning. Thousands of fighters from around the world—including the United States—have traveled to Syria to support oppositionists fighting against the Assad regime and some have connected with extremist groups, including al-Nusra Front. This raises concerns that radicalized individuals with extremist contacts and battlefield experience could either return to their home countries to commit violence at their own initiative, or participate in an al-Qaeda directed plot aimed at Western targets outside Syria.

Lebanon

We expect that one of the continuing effects of the Syrian conflict will be the continued erosion of Lebanese stability this year. The primary drivers of instability in Lebanon are economic, social, and sectarian tensions fueled by the Syrian conflict and Hezbollah's willingness to use violence to protect its own and Iranian interests in Syria. The influx of nearly 1 million refugees from Syria into Lebanon—roughly 20 percent of Lebanon's population prior to the Syrian war—is also straining the country's fragile economy and overburdening already strained public services, particularly in the north and the Beqaa, areas hosting the majority of the refugees.

In May 2013, Hezbollah publicly admitted that it is fighting for the Syrian regime and its chief, Hassan Nasrallah, has framed the war as an act of self-defense against Western-backed Sunni extremists, whom he claimed would target all Lebanese if the Assad regime fell. Hezbollah is sending capable fighters for pro-regime operations and support for a pro-regime militia. Additionally, Iran and Hezbollah are leveraging allied Iraqi Shia militant and terrorist groups to participate in counteropposition operations. This active support to the Assad regime is driving increased Sunni extremist attacks and sectarian unrest in Lebanon.

Following the group's public confirmation that it was fighting in Syria and had played a pivotal role in pro-regime operations in Al Qusayr, Sunni extremist and terrorist elements began a violent campaign of attacks against Hezbollah strongholds in Lebanon. There has been a sharp rise in Sunni extremism in Lebanon over the past 2 years, particularly in the north. Given the character and structure of these many diverse extremist groups there is increasing concern about their threat to Lebanon's stability. In addition there are regular reports of the movement of fighters and trafficking of arms and explosive materials across the Lebanese border with Syria.

- May 2013—rocket attacks against Hezbollah suburbs of Beirut;
- June 2013—Supporters of Salafi leader Ahmad al-Assir attack a LAF checkpoint near Sidon, killing three soldiers; LAF responds by conducting operations against up to 300 al-Assir supporters;
- July–August 2013—Sunni extremist groups, the 313 Brigade and the Aisha Mother of Believers Brigade, each conduct a VBIED attack in Hezbollah-controlled neighborhoods in Beirut (20 dead, over 250 wounded);
- October 2013—LAF seizes a VBIED with 250 kg of explosives and a suicide belt; two soldiers and two armed men killed in ensuing gunfire exchange;
- November 2013—Sunni extremists are tied to two near-simultaneous suicide bombings against the Iranian Embassy in Beirut, probably motivated by revenge for Iran's support of Hezbollah and the Assad regime (25 dead, over 150 wounded);
- January/February 2014—Sunni extremists conduct several VBIED and suicide attacks against Hezbollah and Shia interests in Beirut and Hermel (41 dead, over 280 wounded).

Hezbollah also uses violence to intimidate and kill political rivals, putting Lebanon's stability at further risk and undermining the country's rule of law. The group was most likely responsible for the December 2013 assassination of senior Lebanese official Muhammad Chatah—a longtime critic of the group and former Ambassador to the U.S., who was the diplomatic advisor to former Prime Minister Saad Hariri [killed in a Vehicle Born Improvised Explosive Device].

In short, the various factors contributing to instability in Lebanon are only exacerbated by the protracted conflict in Syria, particularly as tensions grow between Shia and Sunni groups operating inside Lebanon.

Iraq

In Iraq, we have witnessed over the last 3 years a disturbing resurgence by ISIL. The group has a core cadre of veteran leaders, and access to a steady flow of both weapons and fighters from Syria. ISIL is also able to draw from a significant pool of terrorist fighters previously imprisoned by the Iraqi Government. The Syrian conflict has facilitated a greater two-way sharing of Sunni extremists and resources between Syria and Iraq that has contributed to ISIL's increased pace of high-profile attacks.

In 2012, ISIL launched a campaign to free detained members that led to the release of hundreds of prisoners to bolster their ranks. Last year, ISIL's suicide and car bomb attacks returned to their peak levels from 2007–2008. At the end of 2013, the group was averaging a suicide attack each day. The increasingly permissive security environment has allowed ISIL to challenge Iraqi security forces, most recently and notably in Fallujah and Ramadi.

On January 1 of this year, convoys totaling approximately 70–100 trucks with mounted heavy weapons and antiaircraft guns entered the central cities of Fallujah and Ramadi. They quickly secured vital transportation nodes and destroyed most police stations. The Iraqi Army units in the vicinity engaged some armed vehicles but chose to not get drawn into an urban fight. A combination of military, political, and tribal efforts in Ramadi have begun to show results, with the city becoming increasingly secure. The situation in Fallujah, however, is far more disconcerting.

In Fallujah, hundreds of ISIL fighters have joined ranks with former insurgent groups to consolidate control of the inner city and contest areas in neighboring towns. The Iraqi Army is facing significant resistance, including well-trained snipers armed with 50-caliber rifles. Last month approximately a dozen Iraqi soldiers were captured near Fallujah. The next day they were executed. At the moment it remains a tense standoff as some tribes are ready and preparing to fight against ISIL, others are preparing to fight with ISIL, and still others on the fence, waiting to see which side is likely to prevail in the end.

ISIL's strength again poses the credible threat to U.S. interests in the region that it had at its peak in 2006. It has pledged its resources to support establishing hardline Islamic governance. And although ISIL is primarily focused on its activities in Iraq and Syria, it still perceives the United States as an enemy.

Early this year, ISIL publicly claimed its first attack in Lebanon and promised more, demonstrating its aspirations go beyond Syria and Iraq. Also in January, ISIL's leader [Abu Bakr al-Baghdadi] publicly called for operatives in Iraq to surge attacks in Shia areas the group wants to control to inflame to sectarian violence. In the same speech, he threatened ''direct confrontation'' with the United States. In sum, our concerns with the threat posed by ISIL to our interests in the region are currently growing, not diminishing. In the period ahead, we will be watching closely to see if the Iraqi Government's counterterrorism efforts will gain greater traction against the extremist threat.

ADDRESSING THE SPECIFIC THREAT FROM SYRIAN FOREIGN FIGHTERS

At NCTC, in addition to analyzing and assessing threat information, we play an important role in supporting the effort to watchlist known or suspected terrorists. On behalf of the Intelligence Community, NCTC hosts and maintains the central and shared knowledge bank on known and suspected international terrorists and international terror groups, as well as their goals, strategies, capabilities, and networks of contacts and support. This database of terrorism information, known as the Terrorist Identities Datamart Environment (TIDE) supports the border and aviation screening efforts of our partners at the FBI and the Department of Homeland Security. In light of the large foreign fighter component to the Syria crisis that I highlighted earlier, this effort to gather every bit of available information about terrorist identities is particularly important.

For some time we have been engaged in a focused effort—working closely with the Department of Homeland Security and the Federal Bureau of Investigation and our other Intelligence Community partners—to track the travel of any individuals that we've identified as having traveled to Syria to participate in extremist activity. When we obtain such information, we ensure that the individuals in question are added to the TIDE database and that their identifying information is exported to our partners to support their various watchlisting activities. We also work with a wide array of foreign partners to try and learn more about how extremists are, in fact, traveling to Syria, what routes they are using, what facilitation networks are supporting them, and what happens to those extremists both inside Syria and after they leave the battlefield to return to their place of origin. As the conflict in Syria continues, issues associated with Syrian foreign fighters and their travel patterns will be a continued area of the highest priority and emphasis for NCTC and the Intelligence Community.

CLOSING

Members of the committee, the deteriorating situation in Syria, Lebanon, and Iraq is of great concern to the United States and its allies. The potential for further escalation of sectarian violence and the resulting second and third order effects is of tremendous concern to the intelligence community.

Let me assure you that we are also focused intensively on the tactical threat environment in this volatile region and our responsibility to identify and disrupt threats to our personnel serving in these crisis zones. We ask much of our military members, our intelligence service professionals, and our diplomats to operate in such a dangerously unpredictable environment, but I think all of us recognize that it is in our national security interests to operate in these areas.

The National Counterterrorism Center will continue to support our whole-of-government effort in the region by identifying and analyzing threat information and sharing that information with our partners across the government. In addition, we will continue to focus on identifying individuals who might seek to return from these overseas battlefields and do us harm so that our law enforcement and intelligence officials can engage in the appropriate disruption efforts. And throughout we will continue to keep the Congress fully and currently informed of our activities, as required by the law.

On behalf of the men and women of the National Counterterrorism Center, I want to thank you for inviting me to testify, and I look forward to answering any of your questions.

The CHAIRMAN. Thank you all for your testimony. There is a lot of ground to cover here, so let me start.

Mr. Secretary, while we are focused on the Ukraine, I wonder whether the administration is of the view, as some of us are, that the international norms that you talked about in your opening statement and the challenge to international norms and how we respond to that is critically important far beyond even the Ukraine.

Senator Cardin and I were talking yesterday about the consequences of how we respond when other countries like China look to see what we are going to do as they consider their options in the South China Sea, North Korea in terms of its march to weaponization, those places like Africa and the Congo that decide whether or not the international community is going to be responsive or whether they are going to rearm and continue to have millions of lives lost, even as we negotiate with Iran, at the same time that Iran, as we have heard here, is in the midst of promoting, still promoting vigorously, terrorism.

So it seems to me that you need to say what you mean and mean what you say. In that respect, do we understand that this is a challenge in the immediacy about Ukraine, but it is also a broader challenge as it relates to the message that we and our Western allies send globally?

Ambassador BURNS. Thanks, Mr. Chairman. I agree fully with your point. I think there is a great deal that is at stake in Ukraine today. It is about Ukrainians and their ability to make their own choices. It is about Europe and Eurasia. But it is also about the wider consequences that you just described. So I think it is very important for the United States to make clear, as you said, that we will put actions behind our words, about our concerns about what has happened, about the importance of abiding by international norms, again not just for the sake of Ukraine, important as that is, but given the wider stakes that are involved, and it is also important that we work closely with our allies and partners to reinforce the same point, and that is what we have been spending a lot of time and energy doing in recent days, and we will continue to.

The CHAIRMAN. Now, with reference to the Ukrainian situation, I know the Secretary, Secretary Kerry, and his European counterparts met with the Russian Foreign Minister in Paris yesterday. The Russians, at least at this point, will not speak directly to the Ukrainians. What do we envision as to the willingness of Russia to find a diplomatic exit here, and what are the necessary ingredients to deescalate the crisis?

Ambassador BURNS. Mr. Chairman, you know, the essence I think of any deescalatory political process is direct dialogue between the Ukrainian Government and the Russian Government which is aimed at restoration of Ukraine's sovereignty and territorial integrity. The Russian Government has expressed concerns about ethnic minorities, Russian-speaking minorities in eastern Ukraine and in Crimea. We believe, as the Secretary and the President made very clear, that those are unfounded. There is no evidence for any persecution of those minorities. But there are ways of addressing that concern directly with the government in Kiev and also through organizations like the OSCE, which is why we are supporting the sending of monitors from the OSCE to eastern Ukraine and to Crimea to try to establish what the facts are.

So again, as I said, the essence of any kind of diplomatic off-ramp has to be direct dialogue between the Ukrainian Government and the Russian.

The CHAIRMAN. They reject that, at least at this point. Obviously, there is a purpose for the Russians trying, not that I believe it is legitimate, but trying to undermine the legitimacy of the present Ukrainian Government. In a series of international forums they can make the argument, falsely, but they can make the argument.

So my concern is that at some point, from my own perspective, as much as we seek to deescalate this, we have seen this picture before. We have seen what President Putin did in Georgia, in South Ossetia, and other parts. We see him doing it in the Crimea. How serious do we believe is his desire to go beyond Crimea and into eastern Ukraine?

Ambassador BURNS. It is difficult to predict, and we are certainly doing everything that we can with our partners to make clear the costs of any such move. As I said, we are trying to establish OSCE monitors in eastern Ukraine to beat back the false accusation that there is persecution of ethnic minorities going on there. I think the new Ukrainian Government has done a good job of making clear its concern about Ukrainian citizens, west and east, across the whole country. So I think we need to continue to push those lines of effort, and also make clear, as we did today in the actions that the President has taken, that there are costs, and to build patiently, persistently, and firmly counterpressure against what the Russians have already done and making clear that there will be costs if they escalate further.

The CHAIRMAN. Well, I hope that as we pursue the diplomatic course we are organizing as much as possible the international community in joining us in the strongest possible response, because otherwise Putin's calculations will take him to as far as he thinks he can get away with.

Let me just turn quickly to Syria. I heard what you said, but I question whether or not we are fully committed to changing the battlefield equation, because unless, as this committee voted quite some time ago in a bipartisan fashion to arm the vetted Syrian moderate rebels, nothing will change in Assad's equation or against Russia and their patronizing of Assad, for him to feel that he has to do anything but to continue to hang in there and try to win a war of attrition.

So how robustly are we ready to engage in helping to change that battlefield equation, even though it is a lot harder now than it was then? But listening to all the threats that the Director talked about, I just do not see that, unless we do that, we are going to get in a position where we have anything but the potential of a failed state and the consequences of what that that means to our national security, in addition to the bloodshed that is being shed every day in Syria.

Ambassador BURNS. Mr. Chairman, just as you said, there are huge and growing risks, I think, in Syria and in the spillover of Syria's violence into the wider region. We are looking actively at further ways in which we can support the moderate opposition. As you know, we are also trying to intensify cooperation with other backers of the moderate opposition.

The Saudi Minister of Interior, Mohamed bin Nayaf, was in Washington recently and I think we have improved the cooperation and coordination with some of the other backers of the moderate opposition to ensure both that they get the support they need, but also that extremists are denied the funding and the flow of arms that are enabling them to increase their strength. So part of it is what we do; part of it is what we can work with our partners to do.

The CHAIRMAN. Well, I get a sense that we are not as robust as we should be, and, unless we are, we are not going to change the equation in Syria, which means that we are in for a world of hurt as we move forward.

Finally in this regard, this committee gave the President the authorization for the use of force, which I think was a critical element of his ability to at least pursue the chemical weapons issues that Syria possesses. But they have missed two deadlines already. I now see a report where they are accelerating—allegedly accelerating—but accelerating without actually doing anything is inconsequential. To say you are going to accelerate on paper is one thing, but they have missed deadlines.

How convinced are we that we are going to get the commitment of action by the Syrians as it relates to getting rid of their chemical weapons stash?

Ambassador BURNS. Mr. Chairman, the foot-dragging by the Syrian regime has been deeply frustrating. The last few weeks there has, as you rightly pointed out, been an increase in movement in the right direction. By the beginning of next week, I understand that about 35 percent of the chemical materials will have been removed from Syria. So I still think it is possible to meet the 30th of June deadline that has been set for removal and destruction. But we are going to have to keep pushing very hard to ensure that this process continues.

As I said, there has been some accelerated movement in recent weeks, but I do not think we can take that for granted. We need to keep pushing very hard.

The CHAIRMAN. Well, I think we need to keep pushing, and at some point we need to suggest that our patience is not unlimited with constant violation of deadlines that ultimately need to be met. Senator Corker.

Senator CORKER. Thank you, Mr. Chairman.

I did not hear your first questions. I hope I am not being redundant, but I do want to talk a little bit about Syria.

The CHAIRMAN. You are never redundant.

Senator CORKER. Okay, good. Thank you.

In the Syrian issue, I know that it sounds like the chairman and you had a little discussion about that. First of all, I appreciate the work you are doing in counterterrorism and certainly what our Defense is doing relative to some of the regional threats that we have that, candidly, did not need to exist. But they now do because of our inaction and others.

But what is it that we are expecting to do to change the equation on the ground in Syria now that it has become what it is? I do not know if you have got policy moves. I know Secretary Kerry, I saw him a few weeks ago in Europe. He told me he was on the verge of announcing something. We keep hearing that. We have private conversations with others. But there is no balance change that we are seeing.

So what is it that the administration believes is going to be the thing that causes Assad to want to negotiate his leadership away from Syria?

Ambassador BURNS. The reality, just as you said, Senator Corker, is that without a change in Assad's calculation and a change in the balance on the ground it is unlikely, in fact impossible, that you are going to see diplomatic progress, whether it is in Geneva or anyplace else. We are looking actively, as Senator Kerry said to you, at ways in which we can step up our own support for the moderate opposition, which has had more than its share of challenges in the last couple of years.

We are also working I think more effectively with some of the other partners. The Saudis I mentioned earlier in response to the chairman.

Senator CORKER. So are we thinking about lethal support? We have people dropping barrel bombs. Are we thinking about doing something to diminish their ability to do that? I know that there have been debates about title 10 support, having actual military training, having actual military—not our boots on the ground, but our ability to get weaponry and training to the vetted moderates. Are we still looking at that?

Ambassador BURNS. We certainly are still looking at a range of options, some of which I ca not really discuss in this kind of a setting. But we are looking—we understand the urgency of the situation. I think all of us understand what is at stake here, not just for Syria but for its neighborhood, and some of our closest partners are in that neighborhood. So we are looking at what more we can do, but also at what our partners can do more effectively to support the moderate opposition and begin to try to change the realities on the ground.

Senator CORKER. You understand we have been hearing this for years now. And since we first began hearing this, I would guess 100,000 people have died since we first began hearing this.

What is it within the administration right now that keeps the administration from really wanting to put something forth? I mean, do we not have the partnerships we had before in the region? What is the factor that you think keeps our administration from being slightly more forward? I will say this: Things have changed. I think the options that were great options a year ago are probably not as great today. They are just not, because of the extremists that have moved into the region.

But who are our partners now in this effort, our real partners? And what is it that you think keeps the administration from wanting to change that balance on the ground? Have we decided now that we are better off with Assad in place because the extremists are actually worse for our own homeland security than Assad being there? I would just like an explanation because we have been hearing this—100,000 people ago we were hearing this.

Ambassador BURNS. I remain firmly convinced, and the administration does, that Assad is a magnet, as my colleagues were talking about, not only for foreign fighters and violent extremism, but that as long as Assad remains the civil war will continue and get worse and the dangers of spillover get worse as well. So I do not think either our analysis or our resolve has changed a bit on that.

There is more that we can do with our partners. I mentioned the Saudis earlier. The President, as you know, at the end of March is going to be going to Saudi Arabia. We work very effectively, as Derek was describing, with the Jordanians, and I know King Abdullah had a chance to meet with you recently and discuss both his concerns and his plans. We are intensifying our cooperation with Jordan as well.

So this is going to require an all-of-the-above effort, looking at what more we can do, but also what more our partners can do, recognizing the urgency of the situation.

Senator CORKER. Generally speaking, I just want to say it is kind of none of the above. I know there is limited activity that gets discussed in other settings. But I was just in Saudi Arabia not long ago. I can tell you they are one frustrated group of folks at us saying we are going to do something and not doing anything. They obviously went outside the umbrella. There has been some backlash there, I understand.

But it is very disappointing, year after year, 100,000 people later, to continue to hear the same things and yet no action be taken, and I know the situation is much worse now.

Let me ask you this. On Russia, has there been any discussion—and I know that people on both sides of the aisle have discussed energy issues, and I know we are going to talk about sanctions, and we are going to have some economic relief, hopefully, coming next week—is there any discussion right now about our energy policy and additional pressure that might be placed on Russia by moving quickly with that, not again waiting a year but moving quickly with some changes in how we deal with some of our energy issues that might put additional economic pressure on Russia?

Ambassador BURNS. Well, Senator, as you and other members of the committee know very well, the shale revolution and the transformation of the global energy market gives the United States a great deal of strategic leverage we did not have before, and it creates opportunities for us to help the Europeans loosen their dependence on Russian gas, and over the long term gives us strategic assets that I think can be very important in foreign policy.

We need to be very conscious of that as we look ahead and very conscious of that in terms of what it means for our relative strengths and Russia's relative weaknesses as you look out over the next few years.

So to answer your question; yes, people are looking very carefully at that as an element of broader strategy.

Senator CORKER. I think most of the people that look at this issue, much like we could have done some things in Syria a year ago, 2 years ago, and things would not be the way they are today, people look at this energy issue and I think they say, well, if we wait a year or two to announce some things or do some things, it is not going to have the impact that it would have today. So I hope we do not go through the same process in looking at energy that we have in Syria.

I will just close with this. I know my time is up. I think our foreign policy credibility is close to shot at this time. The series of events that have happened over this last year I think have weakened us substantially. Again, I know you are implementers, not setters, and I am not directing this at you.

On Iran, though, I think we all support the diplomatic activities that are taking place there. I think many of us are concerned about the interim deal being the final deal or having a series of rolling interim deals. I would just say that, look, Russia has been our partner in all of these things, and I think us rushing to some agreement that again is not one that is substantial enough will shoot all credibility that we have relative to foreign policy issues.

I would just urge you to—I would urge the State Department, I would urge those that are negotiating, to please pause. Let us make sure that what we do there is something of long-term significance that matters, and let us—certainly, do not appear to be rushing into a deal just to make a deal, which I think that has hurt us over the course of the last year.

I thank you for your service.

The CHAIRMAN. Senator Cardin.

Senator CARDIN. Well, Mr. Chairman, first of all, thank you very much for holding this hearing.

Secretary Burns, it is always a pleasure to have you before our committee, and the other panelists. Senator Corker and I share many common visions on foreign policy objectives, including in Iran and Syria and Ukraine. I disagree with your assessment. I think this administration has shown incredible leadership and effective coalition-building to deal with some extremely challenging problems around the world. It is important that we work as closely as we can together, and I want to talk about the Ukraine specifically.

We have talked about this before, but I am just going to underscore how dangerous this situation is and how Russia is violating not just one, but numerous international obligations. They are violating the OSCE core principles, the 1994 Budapest Memorandum—signed by the United States, United Kingdom, Russia, and Ukraine—the 1997 Ukraine-Russia bilateral treaty, the U.N. Charter.

Russia's military invasion is a gross violation of the Vienna Documents Confidence and Security-Building Mechanisms, which govern military relations and arms control. I could go on and list many, many other international agreements that are clearly being violated by Russia in Ukraine.

Ukraine has shown remarkable restraint. I commend them for being able to put the spotlight on who is the villain here, and it is clearly Russia.

The OSCE has a mechanism in order to deal with it. They have observers. Ukraine has asked those observers to go to Crimea so that we can have objective accounts, because I think it is clear to the world that Russia's justification for what they are doing does not exist.

Mr. Chairman, it is very interesting that those observers have been denied entrance into Crimea by people dressed up in military uniforms and by others who are unidentified. Clearly, we know who is responsible for those denials.

The OSCE media freedom representative and her staff were temporarily blocked from leaving a hotel in Crimea where she had meetings with journalists and civil society activists. The U.N. special envoy was accosted by unidentified gunmen after visiting the naval headquarters. I could go on and on and on about how Russia is denying international institutions that are available in order to deal with this the access they need, which is only accelerating this problem.

As the chairman pointed out, this is an issue that goes well beyond Ukraine and Russia. From the western Balkans to the South China Sea, we have territorial issues in which we worry about military force being used rather than direct bilateral discussions.

So I am proud that the United States has taken a strong position on this and our President has taken a strong position on this. The Executive order that was issued I think is the right course. We are going to have to do more, as you have acknowledged.

But here is the challenge. What is the EU doing? What is the United Nations doing? We have heard a little bit about OSCE. We have heard a little bit about NATO. But I tell you, we have not heard the strong unified voice that we hoped we would see around the world to demand that Russia get out of Ukraine and allow Ukraine to run its own internal affairs.

Where are we with the U.N.? Where are we with the other international organizations and the EU?

Ambassador BURNS. Thanks, Senator. On the EU, as you know, there is an EU summit, an extraordinary EU summit that is going on right now. The President and Secretary Kerry have been in very close touch with EU leaders over the course of recent days. The EU has taken some steps, both——

Senator CARDIN. Are they as broad as what the President has taken on this Executive order?

Ambassador BURNS. They have taken some steps against Ukrainian individuals which are consistent with the Executive order, and I know they are considering today as we meet here a range of other steps. I do believe that EU leaders understand what is at stake here.

Senator CARDIN. As I understand the President's Executive order, it goes beyond just Ukrainians.

Ambassador BURNS. Yes, sir. But as I said, I believe the EU is considering very seriously a range of other steps that it can take. I do agree with you; I think acting as part of a broad international coalition on issues like this is likely to have more significant effect on Russian behavior. So we are going to continue to do everything we can, working with our partners in the EU, to make clear the costs, not only of what Russia has already done, but the increasingly significant costs of any further escalation.

I do believe that EU leaders understand that and are going to act on it.

Senator CARDIN. How about beyond the EU?

Ambassador BURNS. You mentioned the OSCE, sir, which you know very well. OSCE has moved quickly to organize observers in eastern Ukraine. They have run into difficulties in Crimea, but we are going to continue to push that as hard as we can. It is one of the most effective ways to demonstrate the falsity of some of the claims that Russian leaders have made about what is going on in eastern Ukraine and the false accusations about persecution of ethnic Russian minorities there.

So in the U.N. Security Council we will continue to try to keep a focus on the issue as well. So that we will use every international fora that we can to not only highlight our concerns, but build practical pressure on Russia to restore Ukraine's territorial integrity and sovereignty.

Senator CARDIN. Thank you.

The CHAIRMAN. Senator Risch has deferred to Senator Johnson.

Senator JOHNSON. Thank you, Mr. Chairman.

Secretary Burns, can you tell me exactly how the administration views Russia? I would like to think Russia is a friendly rival as opposed to an unfriendly adversary. What is the viewpoint of the administration right now toward Russia?

Ambassador BURNS. Our relationship with Russia is a complicated one. There are some areas in which as a practical matter we have been able to work together in recent years. Afghanistan is one example. It is been true in some other areas as well. But there are also areas of obvious difference, certainly most obviously and most seriously in Ukraine now. But it has been true in other parts of Russia's neighborhood, Georgia, as was mentioned earlier.

And we continue to have serious concerns about human rights abuses within Russia itself. So the honest answer is that our relationship is a mix of areas of obvious difference and in some cases competition and some areas in which objectively we can work together. But right now I think we are in a very difficult period in our relationship with Russia because of Russian behavior.

Senator JOHNSON. In areas, for example Afghanistan, maybe there is a little bit more cooperation there. Then you look at Syria. When we are attempting to work with them as, let us say, partners, do you believe they are always operating with the United States in good faith or are they being duplicitous? I mean, it may be good faith in Afghanistan, there is maybe some shared interests, but more duplicity in Syria?

Ambassador BURNS. I think on Syria we have been frustrated by large dimensions of Russian behavior and actions. On the chemical weapons issue, we have managed to work together and made at least some progress toward the destruction of Assad's chemical weapons stockpile, which objectively, I think, is a good thing for Syria and for the region.

But in other areas we have been frustrated by the reluctance, the unwillingness of the Russian Government to push harder on the Assad regime and to recognize what is at stake, not just for Syria but for the whole region. So Afghanistan, as you mentioned, Russia has played a role in facilitating through the Northern Distribution Network the provision of supplies to the coalition effort in Afghanistan, which again is in a hard-nosed way in Russia's interest because it does not have an interest in the spillover of instability from Afghanistan.

Senator JOHNSON. The Washington Post, in an editorial, said that the administration is basing its foreign policy on a fantasy. Then they changed it in the printed version. But have the events in the Crimea and the Ukraine—is the administration now looking a little more realistically long term?

Ambassador BURNS. Senator, I think, and I have spent a good bit of my own career serving in Russia and working on United States-Russian relations, and I have always tried to be realistic about where there are areas of cooperation, trying to take advantage of that, but also to be honest with ourselves about those areas of obvious difference.

So I think over the long haul we need to be mindful, as I said in my opening remarks, of our own strengths and the strengths of the United States and our partners and the dilemmas that Russia is going to face over the long term.

Senator JOHNSON. I have heard a number of people say that Russia's move in Crimea signals a certain level of weakness on the part of Russia. It looks like a pretty strong move to me. Can we just—you talked about strengths. What gives Russia the strength to do what it did? Why did they think they can do that with impunity?

Ambassador BURNS. Well, given the geography and the proximity of Russia to Crimea and the relative strength of the Russian military compared to the Ukrainian military, it is clear to see how Russia could have——

Senator JOHNSON. So military. But also, is it not their oil?

Ambassador BURNS. Certainly the Russian economy is largely dependent on hydrocarbons, on oil and gas.

Senator JOHNSON. Is it safe to say that high oil prices, which are sometimes driven higher by chaos for example in the Middle East, does that give Russia strength?

Ambassador BURNS. Certainly high energy prices have fueled Russian economic growth in recent years. But that growth has tapered off. It is now under 2 percent in the last couple years, as I recall. As I mentioned earlier, if you look at the way in which the global energy market is being transformed by the shale technology revolution, over the long haul those relative strengths of Russia I think are going to diminish. And Russia has not taken advantage of the opportunity in the last decade to diversify its economy.

Senator JOHNSON. So we are getting right to the point I wanted to get to. You mentioned that we need to remain steady, determined, patient, resolute. The chairman said we have to say what we mean and mean what we say. In other words, not only just talk ???to??? talk; walk the walk. So is this administration going to start looking at Russia with their eyes wide open, understand the reality of the situation, understand the brute force, the lawlessness, the duplicity of Russia? And are we going to start laying in a ratcheted-up level of strategy of increasing the sanctions, increasing the costs, if Vladimir Putin continues to do this? Or are we going to deescalate, provide an off-ramp, and then just kind of hope for the best again?

Do we have a well thought out or are we going to develop a well thought out strategy, understanding the real reality of the situation now?

Ambassador BURNS. Senator, I think we have our eyes wide open about all the realities that you just described. And as I tried to outline in my opening comments, I think we are developing a very careful systematic strategy for dealing with those realities and promoting American interests and values.

Senator JOHNSON. Okay, thank you.

The CHAIRMAN. Senator Shaheen.

Senator SHAHEEN. Thank you.

Thank you all very much for being here at a very challenging time in the world. I am not sure whether this is best directed to you, Deputy Secretary Burns, or Mr. Chollet. But I know that Ukraine is not a member of NATO, but there have been some meetings within our NATO allies to assess the situation in Ukraine. Do we assume that NATO may take a more assertive posture with respect to what has happened there, either rhetorically or in some other ways that symbolically might suggest support for Ukraine?

I wonder if you could talk about what actions we might be taking with NATO to engage their support in the current situation.

Ambassador BURNS. Senator, let me start and then I will turn to Derek. As Secretary Hagel made clear yesterday, we have taken a number of immediate practical steps. We have an aviation detachment in Poland. We are looking to expand cooperation with the Poles through that detachment. There is a NATO air policing unit that operates in the Baltics. We are looking to enhance the contributions that we make there.

So those are steps that are not just symbolic; they are practical and they make clear the commitment of the United States and the entire alliance to partners who have real concerns right now.

Mr. CHOLLET. Senator, if I could add, the North Atlantic Council of NATO has been in continuous meetings over the last week on this issue. I, a week ago today, was with Secretary Hagel in Brussels, where we participated in a NATO Ukraine Commission meeting that was thrown together on very short notice to discuss this crisis, and the Deputy Defense Minister of Ukraine was there.

Today in Brussels the Secretary General of NATO is going to be meeting with the Ukrainian Prime Minister. At each of these junctures, NATO has released very strong statements of support for the Ukrainian people and for the peaceful end to this situation. As the Deputy mentioned, the Baltic air policing mission, which is a NATO mission, Secretary Hagel announced yesterday that the United States, which is currently managing that operation—we have had four F–15s there. We will be adding six additional F–15 today, flying from the U.K. to Lithuania. They will land today and then participate this NATO-led air policing mission for our Baltic partners.

That is reassuring some very critical allies of ours who are made very nervous about the events in the Ukraine and what Russia's been doing.

Senator SHAHEEN. Can you speak to how those actions are being received in Russia?

Mr. CHOLLET. We have been very clear with our Russian counterparts about what we are doing. Chairman Dempsey has had several conversations in the last 48 hours with his counterpart in Russia. We have been very open with them. They are taking this rather matter of factly, to be honest, which is good news. We are not seeking to take an escalatory step vis-a-vis Russia with these moves. We are seeking to reassure some partners who are rightfully nervous about what is going on in Ukraine and what this may mean for them.

So we are very determined to remain transparent. Yesterday, in fact, in Brussels there was a NATO Russia Council meeting that was thrown on the schedule, did not go particularly well, as you might imagine, with the Russian representative there. So NATO is trying to send a clear sign of support and reassurance to NATO partners. We are also trying to be transparent as much as we can with the Russians, so the steps we take to reassure partners do not escalate the situation further.

Senator SHAHEEN. Mr. Olsen, you talked in your testimony about the Islamic State of Iraq and the Levant. Can you talk about the extent to which we think there is collaboration—I do not know if that is the right term—with al-Qaeda on their activities, or how are they directing things that are happening in Iraq and Syria as opposed to al-Qaeda, and how much do we know about them?

Mr. OLSEN. Sure. Senator, the group that you mentioned, ISIL, really is a modification of a prior group, Al Qaeda in Iraq, which was an affiliated group with al-Qaeda. They certainly share that same ideology, although they are now engaged in a rather public controversy about whether ISIL is still part of al-Qaeda, core al-Qaeda under Zawahiri in Pakistan.

But the bottom line is that ISIL is a group that has that same ideology and has been involved in a significant amount of violence both in Syria as well as in Iraq, and has demonstrated really brutal tactics in both locations. As I mentioned, the degree of violence in Iraq, in particular in Fallujah, has risen to a level that we have not seen for several years.

Senator SHAHEEN. Thank you.

My time is up.

The CHAIRMAN. Senator Flake.

Senator FLAKE. Thank you, and thank you all for your service.

Deputy Secretary Burns, with regard to the sanctions announced today, the visa restrictions, how effective do you expect those to be unless our European partners move ahead with some financial sanctions of its own, or sanctions on assets or dealing with assets somehow? What can you tell us about what Europe is doing at this point or the EU?

Ambassador BURNS. Certainly, Senator, I think the steps, both the Executive order that the President signed as well as the visa bans that the State Department is putting into effect, are significant steps. But you are absolutely right, we will have more impact if we do more with our European partners. The EU leaders are meeting right now in an extraordinary summit. I think they are looking very seriously at concrete actions that they can take.

They have taken some already against Ukrainian individuals with regard to travel and asset forfeitures. But they are looking at further serious steps that they can take. So the more we do this in sync with our European partners, the stronger the effect is going to be and that is why we are working quite intensively with our European partners right now.

Senator FLAKE. Thank you. I think the outcry from the United States and from Europe may stop, for the time being at least, Russia from moving further into the Ukraine. But it looks as if they are looking to hunker down pretty quickly in Crimea. They are moving forward with some kind of referendum of elections within a week, and I guess the Russian Parliament is now looking for a way to more easily allow them to be annexed or somehow swallowed up by Russia just in the short term.

Assuming that happens, assuming that Russia tries to give some patina of legality to all of this that way, how long do you think our European allies and others will hold forward with sanctions if Russia does not incur further into the Ukraine, but just settles for Crimea? Will the sanctions regime that we are putting in place be effective in the long term? Will it be held in the long term? What are your feelings there?

Ambassador BURNS. Senator, I would say a couple things. First, I do not think there is any way in which the Russians can put a patina of legality or legitimacy on the referendum that has been discussed. It runs directly counter to the Ukrainian Constitution, which makes clear that any step to alter the territory of the Ukraine has to be approved by an all-Ukraine national referendum.

Second, I think the Europeans understand what is at stake, as I believe we do, and are determined to not only make clear that there are costs of what has already been done, but to increase significantly costs if the situation escalates. I think over the long term what Russia will face if it persists in this is going to be not only increasing costs, but increasing international isolation, which does have a consequence at a moment when Russia has its share of challenges—as I mentioned before, changes in the global energy market, an economy which is not growing at nearly the rate it was before, and a lot of unresolved domestic challenges as well.

Senator FLAKE. I did not say they could put some kind of patina of legality, but they are sure trying.

With regard to Russia and our cooperation with Russia in Syria with regard to chemical weapons, what can you tell us about how the recent events have affected that cooperation with regard to chemical weapons? I am sorry if this is ground you have already plowed here. I came late.

Ambassador BURNS. I will be very brief, Senator. We have been frustrated over recent months by the foot-dragging of the Syrian regime. I believe Russia remains committed to the object here, which is the removal and destruction of all of Syria's chemical weapons stockpile. By the beginning of next week, about 35 percent of that stockpile should be removed from Syria.

It is still possible to meet the 30th of June target that has been set and I think it is vitally important to do that. That is an area where I believe Russia has a self-interest in trying to ensure that that happens. It is not a favor to the United States. It is something that Russia has committed to, and I hope that we can accomplish that goal.

Senator FLAKE. Some of the sanctions that have been talked about or contemplated by the administration and/or Congress involve cooperation or lack thereof or stopping cooperation with Russia on certain issues. How would that impact our ability to carry forward the agreement that we have in Syria?

Ambassador BURNS. It is hard to predict, Senator. But as I said before, I think Russia having made a very visible and public commitment to accomplishing the destruction of Syria's chemical weapons stockpile, I think has a self-interest in trying to ensure that that happens. We will certainly do everything we can to help ensure it does.

Senator FLAKE. Thank you, Mr. Chairman.

The CHAIRMAN. Senator Murphy.

Senator MURPHY. Thank you very much, Mr. Chairman.

Senator Johnson referenced the fact that there are many people who believe that this is actually a sign of Russian weakness. Count me amongst them, in the sense that only 2 weeks ago Russia had the President of the Ukraine essentially under their thumb both economically and politically, a country that had reversed course and had committed into a new economic relationship with Russia, moved away from an economic association with Europe, and today the situation is very different. No matter the future disposition of Crimea, there are 43 million other Ukrainians, which represent 95 percent of the country's population, which now have a government oriented toward Europe, a country—Russia now faces economic sanctions from the United States and Europe that, if not crippling, will certainly be damaging, and he faces a future as somewhat of an international pariah who is going to be much—have a much lesser ability to influence the future course of democratic and economic values.

So ultimately I guess the question is, What is his end goal here? If this was a panicked reaction to Yanukovych's removal from office, then what he is seeking here is not just territorial control of

Crimea, but he is still seeking to influence events in Kiev, that he actually thinks he still has the ability to keep the totality of Ukraine out of the EU and still part of the Russian orbit.

That does not seem to me the direction that this is going. I want to make sure we do everything within our ability through the trans-Atlantic relationship to expel Russian troops out of Crimea. But no matter his ability to cloud the future of Crimea's legal status, I would be interested to hear your take on whether this has anything to do—whether he has any remaining effect on what seems to me now a predestined path of Ukraine into the European?

Ambassador BURNS. Senator, I think the effect if the present events continue on their course is going to be largely to solidify Ukrainians around their own commitment to their independence and sovereignty and deepen their interest in connections to the EU and to the West. I think that is largely the effect. I do not think that is the intended effect of what President Putin has tried to do. I think what he looks for is deferential neighbors and to try to ensure that there are governments in place that are going to be deferential to Russian interests.

As I said in my opening remarks, it is one thing to recognize that Russia has legitimate interests in Ukraine for all sorts of reasons, but that does not justify illegitimate actions. I think those illegitimate actions are over the long haul going to isolate Russia just as you said and undermine its ability to influence its neighbors.

Senator MURPHY. There has been all sorts of loose talk on the television news shows about the fact that just because there are ethnic Russians and Russian speakers in Ukraine, in Crimea and eastern Ukraine, that that somehow equates to Russian sympathizers. That frankly is simply not the case in that part of the world, as it is also not the case in many parts of this country that have large numbers of ethnic Russians.

A followup on Senator Shaheen's question regarding NATO. There have been some that have suggested that the move on Crimea is a caution to admit Georgia and Ukraine into NATO, because then of course we would have an article 5 obligation to defend. The other way of looking at it is that it is an advertisement for why we should offer membership to Georgia now, this year, and Ukraine at the appropriate moment, because it would insulate those countries from future Russian encroachment.

That latter view is mine, but how does the administration view the effect of the events of the past several weeks, maybe most immediately on the potential roadmap for Georgia's ascension into NATO?

Ambassador BURNS. Senator, as you know, American policy across administrations has been to support an open door for NATO, and with regard to Georgia to support Georgia's interest in eventual membership with the membership action plan being the next step along the way. That is obviously a decision that has to be taken within the alliance and there is always an active debate about those issues. But American policy has not changed.

Senator MURPHY. Thank you. Finally, this is not a question that needs to be answered. Let me say that I do not necessarily share your optimism about the direction that our European friends are going. I hope that today's summit results in a new commitment to join us in sanctions. I am glad that the administration took these initial steps today. But given the fact that our economic relationship with Russia is about $40 billion in Europe's economic relationship with Russia is $460 billion, if economic sanctions are to have an effect, which I believe they can, this clearly has to be done in conjunction.

This is a test of the trans-Atlantic relationship and we will see what the result is from our European allies in the coming days and weeks.

Thank you, Mr. Chairman.

The CHAIRMAN. Senator Kaine.

Senator KAINE. Thank you, Mr. Chairman, and thanks to the witnesses.

Two comments on Russia and then I want to ask some questions about Syria. I associate myself with the comments suggesting that Russia's move in the Crimea is ultimately a sign of weakness that is likely to lead to bad consequences for Russia. I think they have overplayed their hand in a way that it is going to have dramatically negative consequences for an economy that already has challenges and a political system that is sort of rotten at the top.

Second, I associate myself with the comments raised by folks around the table that we ought to be using our energy resources to accomplish our foreign policy objectives, especially the support of Ukrainian independence. The energy resources that we have give us such a good ability to provide a backstop and help countries wean themselves away from autocratic regimes that they need to be close to because of energy. Whether that is folks who have to purchase from Russia or folks who we have given a waiver to purchase from Iran, we do have an ability now to strategically use our resources to help pull people away from countries that they would rather not be associated with, and we should be looking at that with respect to Ukraine.

Moving to Syria, I recently returned from a trip to Lebanon with Senator King to talk about Syria there, after earlier visits to Turkey and Jordan. We had a hearing about Lebanon that some in the room attended 10 days or so ago, and it was shocking, the magnitude of the challenge, 4 million Lebanese and now over a million Syrian refugees.

But what was even more shocking is as you talk to Lebanese about any issue Syria is the dark star with its powerful center of gravity that warps everything in Lebanon. The Syrian civil war is ultimately the answer to every question. The kids were running two shifts in the Lebanese schools because of Syrian refugees. Water resources, energy resources, tourism, and the economy.

Despite political instability, Lebanon had been somewhat free from the kind of terrorist bombing activity that had been the norm there during the 1980s and some parts of the 1990s. But as soon as Hezbollah decided to go all in for Assad, then Sunni extremists said, okay, we are going to come fight a battle in your neighborhood. And there has been this extremist violence. Senator King and I were heading off to a meeting in downtown Beirut and two suicide bombers exploded themselves outside of an Iranian cultural center.

The Hezbollah activity in Syria has brought more extremist activity into Syria. The topic of this hearing is the spillover effect, and the spillover effect in Lebanon is just absolutely massive.

It strikes me that as we are grappling with what the United States can do there are sort of at least four areas where we can be engaged. Humanitarian aid to Syrian refugees outside Syria, we are the top provider of humanitarian aid in the world. Not that we cannot do more and not that we cannot be calling on other nations to do more, but in terms of who is providing that humanitarian aid we are No. 1 and there is not a close second.

Second and very importantly is humanitarian aid inside Syria. Where there are 3 to 4 million Syrian refugees outside Saudi Arabia, there are 7 million refugees inside Syria who have been displaced. And Russia has been that stone wall against humanitarian aid delivery, aggressive insertion of humanitarian aid inside Syria.

During the Winter Olympics when the light of the world was on them and they did not want to just be the sole pariah blocking humanitarian aid, Russia finally agreed, after vetoing three Security Council resolutions on humanitarian aid, to a Security Council resolution about the delivery of humanitarian aid inside Syria. The first question I want to ask you is, that was done in mid-February. It has not been many weeks since it was done and I think there was like a 30-day reporting requirement. What have you seen in terms of humanitarian aid delivery inside Syria since the U.N. Security resolution?

Ambassador BURNS. It remains a huge problem and we have not seen huge progress since the passage of Resolution 2139. I think it does provide a tool to try to ensure not only that the siege—and it literally is a siege—of certain cities are lifted, and that we can establish humanitarian access. We are working hard at that in support not just of U.N. and other relief agencies, but also pressing the Russians and others who voted for this resolution to help make it a reality.

But I do not want to suggest to you, Senator, that we have seen kind of dramatic overnight progress. But we are going to keep trying to do everything we can to use 2139 to improve the situation.

Senator KAINE. Mr. Chairman, my time is almost up. The other two elements obviously where we can be helpful, that we have to grapple with policy, is along the lines that were in the Foreign Relations Committee's resolution we passed earlier this year about military support, supporting military support to vetted opposition; and finally the diplomacy. While the Geneva talks have been a failure thus far, there is no substitute for them.

Let me just ask you finally, Do you share DNI Clapper's view that the current battlefield situation in Syria is essentially a stalemate that is likely to last a long time without either side being able to claim a decisive victory?

Ambassador BURNS. I do think the civil war is a bloody stalemate right now. The Assad regime controls some parts of the country, but obviously does not control other swaths of the country right now. I think the longer that bloody stalemate continues, the greater the human cost for Syrians, obviously as you just mentioned, but also the greater dangers to the region, for Lebanon but also for Jordan and Iraq.

Senator KAINE. Thank you, Mr. Chairman.

The CHAIRMAN. Senator Markey.

Senator MARKEY. Thank you, Mr. Chairman.

I want to very strongly contest this idea that massive exportation of American energy is going to affect the Ukraine. I want to say this because I believe our greatest strength is our national economy. I think that is what really makes us strong. Because we are strong at home, we are strong abroad.

So the administration has already approved five export terminals which have the capacity to export 5 trillion feet of natural gas. The Energy Information Agency says that just because of that reduction of supply in the United States it could lead to an upward of 50 percent increase in domestic prices here. Well, that is $62 billion a year that is coming out of consumers' pockets in America, manufacturers' pockets in America. That is a $62 trillion tax, this policy, on Americans every year. It would be close to $600, $700 billion over a 10-year period.

Not only that, it is going to slow the conversion from coal-fired plants over to natural gas plants in the United States, because the price of natural gas is going to go so high here. It is going to slow the conversion of oil-run buses and trucks over to natural gas, which is domestically supplied and is low cost, and as a result we are going to continue to import more oil from places we should not be importing oil. It is going to slow our economic recovery because it is a subsidy right now, this low-cost energy into our economy, and except for labor it is the single largest discretionary item.

And moreover, this whole idea that our natural gas is going to the Ukraine is just completely wrong-headed. Rex Tillerson at Exxon Mobil has a fiduciary relationship with his shareholders. The price in China that he is going to get for natural gas is much higher than in the Ukraine. The price he is going to get in South America is much higher than he is going to get in the Ukraine.

Congress and the President do not control where this natural gas goes. It is not Russia, it is not Venezuela. We are a capitalist country. They are going for the highest price, and that is not from Ukraine.

So this is an illusion and we need a national debate here. We have a tremendous economic recovery being driven by this low-cost natural gas. If we are going to lead to a $62 billion a year increase, a tax, I can understand what Rex Tillerson and the American Gas Association want. Their motto is essentially do not let a good crisis go to waste. Let us just argue for more export of this incredibly valuable natural resource.

But I will tell you this. This is a huge price that we pay in weakening America's economy by doing it, and that is our greatest strength. That is what really allows us to stand astride the world. It is our economy. That is what the rest of the world's afraid of. They want to partner with us. That is why the Ukraine wants to move toward the West. It is our economy that makes us attractive to them. It is not our tanks, it is not our jets. It is our economy. That is what those young people want.

So all I can say to you is it is an illusion. It is a free market out there. Our natural gas is not going to the Ukraine. No President, no Secretary of Defense, can direct it that way. It is not going there. We cannot compete with Russian pipelines with high-cost liquefied natural gas that costs $6.00 just to liquefy it, just to cryogenically freeze it.

So I just say that to you, Mr. Secretary. We need a big debate in America, Mr. Chairman, over the economic impacts on our own country if we decide to just disperse this natural gas around the world, helping the Chinese, yes, helping South Americans, yes, but having such a small impact on what is going on in the Ukraine that people will look back and say, what were they thinking; they had an incredible asset that they allowed to be diffused.

Mr. Secretary.

Ambassador BURNS. I guess with regard to Ukraine, I think there is another dimension, as you know better than I do, to helping the Ukrainians lessen their dependence on Russian natural gas, and that is developing their own resources, whether it is shale or in other areas. The Poles have done some very sensible things in recent years along those lines. So I think those are the kind of things that we are working actively to help the Ukrainians on.

I recognize I am no expert on the global energy market, but I recognize what you said about the very important tradeoffs that are involved here, and that has to be a part of the broader debate that you described.

Senator MARKEY. I do not think the analysis has been done. I think people are just throwing this out as some big idea and it does not come from an analysis of the impact on our economy. It does not come from the incredible manufacturing renaissance we have had in America because of low-priced oil and natural gas.

Yes, I would like to go out into the free market and get an extra eight or ten bucks a barrel for American oil. But what does that do for the low-cost American manufacturers and consumers who have access to it here? So this is a big debate for our economy and all I can say is that if we want the petrochemical, fertilizer, manufacturing industry to be reborn here, decamp from China and come back here, energy is one of the biggest single factors. Fifteen bucks an MCF in China, 5 bucks an MCF here in the United States. That is why they are coming back. You want to double it, then you are going to lose your competitive edge and it is really going to hurt us here in America.

So I just want to throw that out, Mr. Chairman. We need a big national debate over this bonanza of shale oil and gas and see how we benefit most as a country. Thank you.

The CHAIRMAN. Thank you. That is 37 years of experience over in the House of Representatives speaking.

Senator MARKEY. By osmosis you pick up a few things.

The CHAIRMAN. I have one final question and I think Senator Corker does.

Senator KAINE. And I do as well, Mr. Chairman.

The CHAIRMAN. Okay.

So, Secretary Chollet, a question and a caution. The question is, In light of what has happened here with Russia and considering the announcements of the Secretary of Defense about our overall plans for the future, does this give us cause to reconsider what we are doing in Europe?

Mr. CHOLLET. In terms of military posture?

The CHAIRMAN. Yes.

Mr. CHOLLET. Well, sir, as you know, we maintain a very robust posture in Europe. Even though we have had to come down since the end of the cold war, we still have many, many forces forward-deployed. I think that the QDR that was released several days ago makes very clear that we still, despite the budget pressures we face, despite a commitment to implement a rebalance toward Asia, that we are privileging the trans-Atlantic alliance and we are going to have the necessary forces and energy in place to continue to work very closely with our NATO allies.

So I think that part of what we are trying to do is build strong partners; work through strong partners. The aviation detachment in Poland that has been mentioned several times already is a perfect example of how the United States, with very little investment, a matter of a few airplanes, can work very closely with our Polish partners both to reassure them and build up their capability to work with us to take care of our common security.

The CHAIRMAN. I appreciate that, the aviation detachment. I think it is a good thing. But it is not a challenge to the Russians if they decided to move further east—further west, I should say. So I just think that it is a moment to think about where we are headed here, because there were some presumptions, I think, and I am not sure that, based on current events, those presumptions do not need to be reviewed.

My caution is that I agreed to arms sales to Iraq after a lot of concerns and a lot of collective work to get to a point that I thought it was propitious to do, but I read these reports of Israelis stopping a ship with dozens of rockets, including Syrian-made M–302s, that as I understand the reports show ultimately came from Iran, went to Iraq, where they were placed on a ship and hidden under cement. The Cubans use sugar. Here they use cement to hide the missiles. And then went down from there to the coast, along the coast of Africa, where it was intercepted.

You know, the Iraqis must understand, whether it is overflights by Iran into Syria or being a place where you can send missiles and then have them boarded on a commercial ship and then trying to evade what I think are violations of international norms in terms of the shipment of missiles here, that that behavior, one, is unacceptable, and two, comes with consequences.

Every time I try to help you move forward, I get a set of circumstances that increase my concern about the Iraqis' commitments. So I just want to caution that as I look at this case, which we will be reviewing, and others that our Iraqi partners must understand that there are consequences in this regard, consequences until we ultimately resettle all of the MEK, to their security. There are a series of things here.

I have been willing to be helpful, but I have to be honest with you: I get concerned when I see actions such as these.

Senator Corker.

Senator CORKER. Mr. Chairman, just on that note, here we are. Again, I think this committee in a bipartisan way has done everything it can to try to support and bolster things that the administration has at least tilted at publicly. Maybe today the fact that we are having a hearing on Syria and we have got our counterterrorism person here because we know what has happened and Syria is now a threat to our Nation, and our Director of National Intelligence has said that, we have our person involved in international defense issues working on the region because we know the region has been destabilized because of lack of followthrough.

I just have to tell you it is disappointing. And again, I really respect the public service of all three of our panelists. It is disappointing that we just continue to have really no policy, no policy in Syria, other than dealing with chemical weapons at a slow pace. So I am just very disappointed. I know it is even more difficult to have a policy because we did not take actions earlier on the that administration itself declared were going to take place.

So anyway, I think this is a telling panel. I appreciate you having this hearing.

I just want to close with this. I think it is an incredible thing that in this Foreign Relations hearing we were able to get the Senator from Massachusetts, who I respect—and I say this with affection—to give a 7-minute oration on the importance of fossil fuels to our economy. So I want to thank you for that and I look forward to that being on YouTube over and over and over again. But I thank you for that.

I would just ask——

Senator MARKEY. Would the gentleman yield as the ranking member?

Senator CORKER. If the chairman will let me, yes, I will.

Senator MARKEY. Those of us who sit down here only get 5 minutes, and it was only 3 of my minutes.

Senator CORKER. Well, it was a great testament to the importance of inexpensive fossil fuels to our economy.

I would just ask, since this is a place where debates usually begin and since I agree we should have a debate, what are some of the dimensions that the State Department is looking at? We understand there are some trade issues, some WTO issues. I realize the complexities are much more difficult than just waving a wand and natural gas appearing in Ukraine. But what are some of the things that are just being discussed, that are not agreed to, relative to how energy policy in our Nation with excesses can help and maybe cause Europeans, candidly, who as someone mentioned earlier do not look like they are acting extremely courageous now because of some of these energy issues and other things—what is it we might do? What are some of the things we might be considering relative to energy that could be important right now relative to Ukraine?

Ambassador BURNS. I think the most important thing we can do, Senator, with regard to Ukraine is continue to help them develop their own energy resources off the Black Sea, for example, take advantage of shale technology, as the Poles have done recently, I think help them to diversify their sources beyond Russia, because there are others in Central Asia and other energy producers to whom they can turn; to help improve energy efficiency, because energy use is enormously inefficient in Ukraine.

So those are all very practical things that I think we can do, quite apart from the broader debate that you have both been talking about, about how does the United States best use what is going to be an enormous asset, I think, in the coming years, already is an enormous asset as a result of the shale revolution.

Senator CORKER. But is there any discussion about that specifically, which is I think what evoked the conversation we had? Are there at least some considerations being made for using this resource that we have today to cause there to be a little change in the balance in Ukraine?

Ambassador BURNS. There certainly is a lot of active strategic consideration being given to how this huge asset might affect strategy and foreign policy. Again, it is going to have to flow from a national debate, which involves tradeoffs in this country. There are a lot of other parts to the executive branch that are going to be involved in this as well as the Congress. But I do think it is going to provide a very significant asset for the United States for many decades to come, and I do think that asset and how we use it is going to have an impact on the leverage of countries like Russia that for many years have used an abundance of hydrocarbons as a tool of national security.

Senator CORKER. So it would be fair to say there are active discussions at high levels within our government relative to how we use this resource, natural gas, today to help us with some of the issues we are dealing with in Europe right now, both their resistance to put in place sanctions and Ukraine itself? There is active discussions at high levels regarding that?

Ambassador BURNS. There certainly is.

Senator CORKER. Thank you.

The CHAIRMAN. Senator Kaine.

Senator KAINE. Just briefly, Mr. Chair. I want to echo—first I have great respect for my Massachusetts colleague's understanding of these issues, and his request that we ought to have a national debate about this I think is very appropriate. I think when that debate is engaged we will find that the position that we should use in a strategic and specific way are assets to accomplish important national security objectives is not based on an illusion or a lack of analysis.

Now, it may at the end of the day be, as the Senator indicated, a matter of tradeoffs. We may see that there are real advantages from it, but the advantages are outweighed by domestic pricing or domestic economic effects. But I know from interaction with nations that are currently in the nations that have received waivers from Secretary Kerry to enable them to purchase Iranian oil, for example—they get a waiver from the sanctions regime because their economies would not allow them to function absent Iranian oil. They are very interested in what tradeoffs they could achieve in purchasing American energy and weakening their reliance on Iranian oil.

That can be a very powerful lever in attempting to find the diplomatic path that we want toward a nonnuclear weaponized Iran. So I think a national debate is a good idea. I think there are going to be tradeoffs. it may end up being the will of Congress that we want to keep everything on shore and not use it in that way. But the suggestion that the believe that this is an asset that can accomplish a national security objective is asserted without analysis or is an illusory one, I think that is going to be proven to be untrue when we get into the debate.

Thank you, Mr. Chairman.

Senator MARKEY. I have a final comment. I would like to do it in 1 minute, Mr. Chairman.

The CHAIRMAN. Okay.

Senator MARKEY. I can do it in 1 minute. I will just say that we are a capitalist country, not a Communist country. Venezuela, Russia, they can direct their oil, their gas, anywhere they want. We cannot do that. We should just accept capitalism. It is going toward the highest price. That is in China and South America. And if we allow for a 50-percent rise in natural gas prices here, the large bus and truck fleet is ready to convert over to natural gas. You need a small number of stations to do it, if it is low-priced. If you just do one-third of that fleet, you cut back by 1 million barrels of oil that we are importing from the Middle East right now.

To a very large extent, the more we become energy independent the stronger the United States is. That is what isolates us right now from any pressure from Russia, is that sense that they do not have any control over our energy situation. We just have to be very careful that we do not miss the opportunity to break total dependence on imported oil. That is what conversion of natural gas from oil-fired buses and trucks allows to happen. It is what a reestablishment of a strong manufacturing base in America allows to happen. It is what—Secretary Kerry said this. Climate change is a huge issue. It is a huge national security issue. The faster we convert over from coal over to natural gas is the sooner we are going to meet our greenhouse gas commitments at Copenhagen and later in Paris.

So I just put it in all those national security contexts and I ask for a real debate, not an illusory debate by foreign policy experts, but economic experts objectively weighing in on this as well.

So I thank you.

The CHAIRMAN. Well, it seems that the debate has been started.

Let me thank this panel for a lot of insights. We may have a little difference here on how we use our energy, but there is no difference, I believe, between us on standing up to Russia's aggression as it relates to the Ukraine and what we need to do in response. I look forward for the committee coming together, as it has so many times, to do that by early next week.

With the thanks of the committee, this panel is excused. Let me call up our second panel. We have with us Daveed Gartenstein-Ross with the Foundation for the Defense of Democracies and Matthew Levitt of the Washington Institute of Near East Policy. We welcome them as we excuse the other panel.

[Pause.]

The CHAIRMAN. Your full statements will be included in the record without objection and we would ask you to summarize your statements in about 5 minutes so that we can engage in the type of dialogue you just saw us engage with our previous panel. So Mr. Gartenstein, I think we can start with you.

STATEMENT OF DAVEED GARTENSTEIN–ROSS, SENIOR FELLOW, FOUNDATION FOR DEFENSE OF DEMOCRACIES, WASHINGTON, DC

Mr. GARTENSTEIN-ROSS. Chairman Menendez, Ranking Member Corker, and distinguished members of the committee, it is an honor to appear before you to discuss the spillover effect of the Syria conflict. At this point the Syria war is likely to continue for a long time. We should not altogether rule out the possibility that Assad's regime could fall unexpectedly fast. The regime could be seriously threatened, for example, of rebel infighting declines and is combined with battlefield reversals or growing defections from the government side.

But nonetheless, it is now clear that Assad's fall is not the inevitability that many analysts believed a year ago and the likeliest scenario is that which the U.S. intelligence community now predicts, which is the war continuing for another decade or more.

Assad's position has been bolstered by two primary factors. One is that he has been heavily supported by both Iran and Russia; and the second is his willingness, brazen willingness, to allow jihadists and other actors viewed as problematic by outside states to flourish relative to other rebels. The Syrian military has not made efforts to prevent jihadist groups, like Jibhat al-Nusra or the Islamic State of Iraq and Al-Sham, or ISIS, from holding territory as it has done for more moderate factions within the opposition. This Machiavellian strategy has served its purpose. The major role jihadists now play has deterred Western countries and others from throwing significant weight behind the opposition.

The war in Syria has already produced tremendous ripple effects and they will only widen. A major ripple is foreign fighters. The impact that the Syria war will have on this generation of jihadists will be every bit the equal of what the Afghan-Soviet War meant for militants who came of age in the 1980s. Both conflicts should be considered first-order humanitarian disasters. Both conflicts have attracted a large number of Sunni Muslim fighters and, unfortunately many foreign fighters have joined jihadist factions.

In the Afghan-Soviet war, relationships amongst militants forged on the battlefield endured for decades and changed the international security environment. They gave birth to al-Qaeda and foreign fighters' roles in many conflicts, such as the extraordinarily bloody Algerian civil war, were significant. Like the Afghan-Soviet war, the Syria war will also have far-flung consequences.

Around 11,000 foreign fighters have been drawn to the battlefield, a number that already rivals the number of Arabs who flocked to South Asia to help the Afghan cause in the 1980s. Director Olsen highlighted European Muslims who travel to Syria to fight Assad and concerns about their liaisons with jihadist groups. A recent study estimates that up to 1,900 of the foreign fighters in Syria hail from Western Europe, and this is now seen as a top national security concern in several western European countries.

However, the impact of foreign fighters is likely to be felt most acutely outside the West. About 2,100 Jordanians have joined the jihad. Over 1,000 Saudis have gone to fight in Syria, at a time when the country is already challenged by natural demographic trends. Put simply, given their population explosion, their oil is buying them less and less relative to their population, which makes it difficult for them to absorb the foreign fighter challenge.

The Afghan-Soviet war shows that foreign fighters can produce consequences in unanticipated places. About 1,000 Tunisians have gone over and Indonesians are for the first time going overseas to fight, not just to train, which has given rise to concerns that this conflict may breathe new life into the group Jemaah Islamiya, which analysts previously considered to be moribund.

My written testimony emphasizes the great spillover we have already seen in two countries, in Lebanon and Iraq. Director Olsen talked about the revitalization of the Islamic State in Iraq and Al-Sham, which is a serious concern. Already the Syria war is a major tragedy and it is likely to have a tragic ending, and the United States is probably unable to avert that even if we choose to become more deeply involved.

At a policymaking level, I would describe the United States response to developments in Syria as confused. I share the frustrations of this panel about our strategic drift in this conflict. We have not defined our desired end state. We seem to vaguely know what we do not want to happen, but have little idea in my view how to get there.

Further, there is the risk that the more involved we choose to be the greater the danger that we will be drawn into the conflict in ways that we do not intend. One priority should be ameliorating the massive humanitarian crisis in the region, something we should do for moral reasons, but also for strategic reasons as the refugee camps and other humanitarian factors can serve as a potential radicalizing element.

It is at least acceptable and perhaps desirable for the United States to provide small arms to rebel factions. It will provide an opportunity to map those factions and also provide the United States with both a presence and a platform. We should, however, resist the temptation to send antitank or antiaircraft weapons to Syrian rebels, which present significant risks that the weaponry could end up in jihadist hands.

An unfortunate reality of the 21st century is that we need to deal with an environment of severely constrained resources, and in Syria it is very difficult to achieve real strategic gains at an acceptable coast at this point.

Thank you for inviting me to testify. I look forward to talking to you during questions.

[The prepared statement of Mr. Gartenstein-Ross follows:]

PREPARED STATEMENT OF DAVEED GARTENSTEIN-ROSS

Chairman Menendez, Ranking Member Corker, and distinguished members of the committee, on behalf of the Foundation for Defense of Democracies, it is an honor to appear before you to discuss the spillover effect of the Syria conflict.

The war in Syria has already produced tremendous ripple effects internationally, and they will only widen over time. The impact the Syria war will have on this generation of jihadists will be every bit the equal of what the Afghan-Soviet war meant for militants coming of age in the 1980s. Both conflicts should be considered first-order humanitarian disasters, justifiably inflaming passions throughout the Muslim world and beyond. Because of the devastation wrought by both wars, the various violent nonstate actors who showed up to defend Muslims against their antagonists gained legitimacy from the clerical class and popularity at the street level. Unsurprisingly, both conflicts attracted a large number of Sunni Muslim foreign fighters from abroad, most of whom were drawn to the battlefield by grisly representations of what was happening and the desire to battle repressive forces who willingly shed innocent blood.[1] Despite the often noble intentions for being drawn to the battlefield, many foreign fighters joined jihadist factions.

In the Afghan-Soviet war, relationships among jihadists were forged on the battlefield that endured for decades and profoundly changed the security environment in many countries: Al-Qaeda (AQ) itself was, in fact, one of the outgrowths of these relationships. But while Communists were the enemy in the Afghan-Soviet war, the Syrian war has taken on a more sectarian hue. Iran has steadfastly supported Syrian President Bashar al-Assad's embattled regime, and the Quds Force, an elite unit within the Iranian Revolutionary Guard Corps (IRGC), has deployed in support of Assad's government. Hezbollah militants and Shia irregular fighters from multiple countries have also entered Syria to support Assad. This dynamic has already produced sectarian ripples that did not exist in the Afghan-Soviet war.

In addition to the foreign fighters who have been drawn to the battlefield—estimated at as many as 11,000 by a recent International Centre for the Study of Radicalisation (ICSR) report[2]—two of Syria's neighbors, Lebanon and Iraq, have been hit particularly hard. The Syria conflict has bolstered Sunni jihadists in Lebanon and reignited sectarian tensions, manifested in shootings on the streets, bombings, and assassinations. Iraq has experienced even more troublesome sectarian violence than Lebanon, and in addition a major Iraq jihadist group, the Islamic State of Iraq and al-Sham (ISIS), experienced a stunning revival due in significant part to events in Syria. ISIS's gains are reflected in more than 7,800 civilians dying in violent attacks in Iraq in 2013 (making it the deadliest year the country has seen since the height of the civil war in 2006–07), and the dramatic offensive the jihadist group launched on January 1 of this year, in which it captured major parts of Fallujah and Ramadi.

A year or two ago it appeared that Assad's regime might collapse quickly, but the situation in Syria can now be described as a stalemate, and the U.S. intelligence community believes the war could ravage the country for another decade or more.[3] Though the possibility of an unexpectedly fast regime collapse should not be ruled out entirely, it is fair to say that a large part of the Assad regime's unexpected longevity can be attributed to two factors: outside support from Iran and Russia, and Assad's extraordinarily Machiavellian strategy. Assad has overwhelmingly concentrated his military resources and efforts on relatively moderate insurgent factions, which has ensured that jihadists play an increasingly prominent role on the rebel side. Regardless of the reprehensibility of the regime's strategy, it has served its purpose: the major role jihadists now play in the opposition has deterred Western countries and others from throwing significant weight behind the rebels. As the Syria conflict continues to rage, the problems associated with it will mount.

The U.S. has yet to match its desired outcome in Syria to the means it is willing to employ in addressing the conflict. This testimony will conclude by contextualizing our consistent failure to match ends to the means we are willing to employ in Syria, and it will suggest both a paradigmatic course and also specific policy prescriptions. The bottom line is that there is little we can do to end or otherwise "solve" the Syria conflict. The best we can do, most likely, is to understand the tremendous ripples that this war is producing, and attempt to contain the spillover.

SYRIA'S ONGOING CIVIL WAR

As the respected Middle East scholar Emile Hokayem has noted, "Syria as the world has known it for the last four decades no longer exists."[4] Yet although his country is fractured, Assad may be able to avoid the collapse of his regime indefinitely.

As I mentioned previously, we should not rule out the possibility that Assad's regime could fall unexpectedly fast. It suffers from the combination of a moribund economy and a hollowed-out military that increasingly relies on conscripts, and the regime could be seriously threatened if rebel infighting declines and is combined with other major trends, such as battlefield reversals or growing defections on the government's side. Nonetheless, it is now clear that Assad's fall is not the inevitability that many analysts believed it to be a year ago, and the likeliest scenario is that which is now envisioned by the U.S. intelligence community: that is, the war continuing for another decade or more. And rather than the conflict ending with a clear winner that controls a unified state, it is entirely possible that it will terminate in "fragmented sovereignty," where a variety of state and nonstate actors are dominant in different areas.[5] Such a possibility is consistent with Director of National Intelligence James Clapper's pronouncement in February 2014 testimony before the U.S. House of Representatives that Syria appears destined for "a perpetual state of a stalemate'' in which "neither the regime nor the opposition can prevail.''

For context on the present shape of the Syria war, Assad's overreactions had much to do with the early escalation of the struggle against him. As revolutionary fervor caught hold in the Arab world, Syria experienced a seemingly limited set of demonstrations beginning on March 15, 2011. The Deraa demonstrations were the most destructive. After a crowd burned down the city's Baath Party headquarters, the regime "responded decisively, driving straight to the heart of the protest movement, the Omari Mosque.''[6] There, the 4th Armored Division fired on unarmed protesters, killing up to 15. Images and video of the slaughter rapidly circulated through opposition media. This early incident is representative of the beginning of the conflict, where the regime's overreactions prompted escalation on the other side.

The regime faced internal and external problems. Soldiers began to defect rather than following orders to shoot protestors. On July 29, 2011, a video posted to YouTube by former Syrian Army officers announced their defection and the formation of the Free Syrian Army. The Syrian Government's excesses and its geopolitical position (Syria was allied with Iran, putting it at odds with the region's Sunni states) caused it to become increasingly isolated, and helped the opposition find sponsors. Following a series of meetings during the summer in Turkey and Qatar with those countries' approval, opposition forces made a further play for legitimacy and recognition by establishing the Syrian National Council (SNC) in October 2011. The SNC "quickly secured Turkish, Qatari and, to a lesser extent, Saudi political and material support.''[7]

The Assad regime's increasing isolation was reflected in the Arab League's decision to suspend Syria in November 2011. Other regional leaders, including Jordan's King Abdullah and Turkish Prime Minister Recep Tayyip Erdoğan, called on Assad to resign.[8]

The opposition was nowhere near as organized as surface appearances may have made it seem. It was, in fact, beset by personality clashes, and failed to reflect Syria's diversity. Nonetheless, the combination of defections, Assad's isolation, and an increasingly potent opposition caused the regime to experience battlefield setbacks. As pressure mounted, the Syrian military both lost territory and also made tactical retreats. Analysts began to see it as inevitably doomed.

By now, however, Assad's regime is embattled and weakened, but has grown likelier to survive—even despite having crossed a U.S. "redline" by using chemical weapons against the opposition in August 2013. It is worth noting three major challenges the regime now confronts. First, Syria is about as isolated internationally as it could be (with the noteworthy exception of the support it receives from Iran and Russia, which will be discussed momentarily). Second, Syria's economy has been severely damaged by the civil war, and multiple reports have portrayed the regime as teetering on the brink of bankruptcy. Third, the military's effectiveness has severely declined due to both attrition produced by the conflict and also significant numbers of defections. As a result, the regime has had trouble taking advantage of recent rebel infighting as an opportunity to regain territory. When it redeployed forces into Aleppo in January, for example, the regime was forced, due to hard limitations on its reliable manpower, "to give up control of the southern city of Jassem and the long-contested Ghouta neighborhood east of the capital, Damascus.''[9]

Despite these weaknesses, Assad's position, and ability to survive, has been bolstered by two primary factors. First, his regime has been heavily supported by both Iran and Russia, both of which see this course as advancing their strategic interests. Iran doesn't want to lose its close ally, while Russia wants to maintain access to its naval base at Tartus, which it views as important to its ability to project power in the Mediterranean.[10] The role both Russia and Iran are playing feeds into the global jihadist narrative in discernible ways: Russian support for Assad conjures the image of external powers imposing tyrants upon the Muslim world, while Iran's role magnifies sectarian animosities. This sectarianism is further increased by the fact that Hezbollah has deployed combatants to support Assad's regime, while Iran has helped to facilitate the entry of Shia irregular fighters from countries like Afghanistan, Bahrain, and Yemen.

A second factor bolstering Assad's chances of survival is his willingness to allow jihadists, and other factions viewed as malign by outside states, to flourish relative to other rebel factions. As previously alluded to, the regime has concentrated its military resources on fighting the more moderate opposition, while allowing extremist groups and other factions widely viewed as undesirables to become relatively strong. While the Syrian military has fiercely fought to recover territory controlled by the Free Syrian Army, it has not made similar efforts to prevent the jihadist groups, Jabhat al-Nusra or ISIS, from holding territory. Further, the regime's pattern of releasing jihadist prisoners—but not those who might join more moderate rebel factions—during the course of the conflict suggests that it views making jihadists a prominent part of the rebellion as more important at this stage than defeating them or thinning their ranks.[11]

Assad appears to have followed a similar pattern with respect to Kurdish groups, undertaking a tactical retreat from northern Kurdish regions near the Turkish border. Given Turkish support for the Syrian rebels, this retreat served a strategic purpose: Turkey has had significant troubles with Kurdish separatism, and Kurdish control of territory in Syria's north raises the possibility that a rebel victory could threaten Turkish territory. Turkey viewed Assad's retreat from Kurdish areas through this lens, as government sources told the media that Syria "deliberately left the three districts on the Turkish border in northern Syria to the control of the Democratic Union of Kurdistan (PYD), known as an affiliate of the outlawed Kurdistan Workers' Party (PKK)," and voiced concerns about a new PKK front opening up inside Syria.[12]

This is extraordinarily Machiavellian strategy has served its purpose. The major role jihadists now play in the Syrian opposition has deterred Western countries and others from throwing significant weight behind the opposition. Syrian democratic activist Haitham al-Maleh has described ISIS, with some justification, as "a mine planted by the Assad regime in the revolution's body to warn the international community of approaching or interfering in Syrian issues."[13]

FOREIGN FIGHTER NETWORKS IN SYRIA

One extraordinarily important aspect of the Syria conflict is the fact that the rebel side is highly popular throughout the Muslim world, and the jihad enjoys deep mainstream clerical support. Regional ulema widely believe that Syria represents a legitimate jihad in support of fellow Muslims, and the fight has been endorsed by such figures as Yusuf al-Qaradawi and Al-Azhar's Sheikh Hassan al-Shafai, and such organizations as Egypt's Muslim Brotherhood. At a Friday sermon in Mecca's Grand Mosque, senior cleric Shaikh Saoud al-Shuraym encouraged congregants to support anti-Assad rebels by "all means." To the extent that the jihad is dominated by salafi jihadists, including al-Qaeda and its fellow travelers, the conflict helps to legitimate them, boost their manpower, and attract financial support to their cause.

The emotional resonance of the conflict and success of the call for jihad can be seen in the enormous number of foreign fighters who have answered the call. As I noted earlier, the number of fighters who traveled to Syria from abroad to fight Assad's regime is estimated to be as high as 11,000, and even that number may be conservative. They have come from a large number of countries—around 50, according to U.S. intelligence assessments.

Earlier, I drew a comparison between the Syria conflict and the Afghan-Soviet war. Similar to the Syria conflict, the rebel side in that conflict was extremely popular throughout the Muslim world, and the anti-Soviet fight was widely endorsed by clerics as a legitimate defensive jihad. Around 10 thousand Arabs flocked to South Asia to help the Afghan cause.[14] The ripple effects of that conflict were tremendous, touching numerous countries. Al-Qaeda itself was a product of the Afghan-Soviet war, founded in August 1988, in the waning days of the conflict.[15] At that time, Osama bin Laden and his mentor, Abdullah Azzam, agreed that the organization they had built during the course of the Afghan-Soviet war to support the fight against Russian occupiers shouldn't simply dissolve when the war ended, but rather its structure should be preserved to serve as "the base" (al qaeda) for future mujahedin efforts.[16] Veterans of the anti-Soviet jihad went on to play a critical role in the Algerian civil war that claimed over 150,000 lives; and the Afghan-Soviet war left behind a wrecked country that would serve as a safe haven for a large agglomeration of jihadist groups. Thus, the ripples of the Afghan-Soviet war could be felt in a large number of far-flung places: while the fact that the conflict would have second-order consequences could have been predicted at the time, the exact reach of the Afghan-Soviet war's ripples was unpredictable.

Similarly, it can be said with certainty that the foreign fighters who have been drawn to Syria will prove to be profoundly important, and their impact on jihadism will likely reach places that analysts don't anticipate at present. One issue worth highlighting is European Muslims who have traveled to Syria to fight Assad's regime: the most comprehensive open-source estimate holds that up to 1,900 of the foreign fighters in Syria hail from Western Europe.[17] The possibility that these individuals could return and either carry out attacks or otherwise foster a militant milieu has made this issue a top national-security concern in several Western European countries.

The percentage of Western foreign fighters who might be expected to carry out attacks against the West is relatively low. In a recent comprehensive study examining foreign fighters in several conflicts, Norwegian researcher Thomas Hegghammer found that "no more than one in nine foreign fighters returned to perpetrate attacks in the West."[18] As Hegghammer details, there are two sides to this finding. First, it is far from true that "all foreign fighters are domestic fighters-in-the-making." But conversely, though this is a low percentage of the whole, it is nonetheless high enough to "make foreign fighter experience one of the strongest predictors of individual involvement in domestic operations that we know." Given the large numbers who have gone to the Syrian battlefield, there is clearly cause to view this as a concern.

But the largest impact of foreign fighters returning to their home countries is likely to be felt outside the West. The ICSR study names Jordan as the largest contributor of foreign fighters to Syria, with about 2,100 having joined the jihad.[19] Several Jordanians serve in prominent leadership roles within Jabhat al-Nusra and ISIS. Nusra's head sharia official is a Jordanian who holds a doctorate in Islamic law from the University of Jordan, and young Jordanians also serve as officials in Nusra's military wing.[20] Combined with the significant Syrian refugee presence in Jordan and consequent strains on the country's economy, returning foreign fighters could have a drastic impact on Jordan.

ICSR names Saudi Arabia as the second-largest contributor of foreign fighters in Syria, with over a thousand. Other estimates are even higher, ranging up to 3,000.[21] Saudi Arabia implemented a set of policies toward Syria early in the civil war that can only be described as short-sighted and potentially suicidal: it offered to commute the sentences of its prisoners on the condition that they go to Syria to fight Assad's regime.[22] More recently, Saudi Arabia has indicated that it will clamp down on its citizens traveling to Syria to join the jihad. However, the monarchy has a pattern of taking one step forward and two steps back in fighting jihadist militancy, and also is heavily invested in defeating Assad's regime. Thus, it is worth watching whether Saudi Arabia ends up deviating from its announced policies designed to stem the flow of citizens to Syria. Unfortunately for Saudi Arabia, its foreign fighters will be returning at a time when the country is experiencing increasing challenges based on natural demographic trends: Put simply, as its population grows, the country's oil wealth provides them fewer and fewer benefits. As Saudi Arabia experiences increasing financial problems, its ability to simply throw money at problems erodes, and thus it becomes more difficult to absorb such challenges as large amounts of returning foreign fighters.

ICSR's study names Tunisia as the third-biggest contributor of foreign fighters, with about 970 Tunisians traveling to Syria; there are also higher estimates. The jihadist group Ansar al-Sharia in Tunisia has frequently posted notices of the martyrdom of Tunisians killed in Syria, and videos posted to YouTube are testament to the Tunisian presence in that conflict. Tunisia is a small country, and though the current challenge it faces from jihadist groups has been low in intensity, it may be vulnerable if it proves unable to absorb returnees.

As the Afghan-Soviet war demonstrates, the ripples of jihadists being drawn to major conflicts can also occur in unanticipated places. A recent report by the Institute for Policy Analysis of Conflict (IPAC) notes that, in Syria, Indonesians are for the first time "going overseas to fight, not just to train, as in Afghanistan in the late 1980s and 1990s, or to give moral and financial support, as in the case of Palestine."[23] Currently the number of Indonesians in Syria is relatively small, estimated at around 50 by Indonesia's Foreign Ministry. Nonetheless,the Indonesian presence in Syria has raised fears that the conflict may breathe new life into Jemaah Islamiyah (JI), which analysts previously considered moribund due to Indonesian security forces' crackdown against it. IPAC's report notes that the Syria war has already bolstered JI's prestige: when jihadists groups are at the forefront of a popular conflict, they will reap the benefit. Moreover, 20 Rana al-Sabbagh, "Jordan Faces Growing Salafi-Jihadist Threat," Al-Monitor, Feb. 4, 2014. IPAC suggests that the Syria conflict could magnify sectarian tensions in Indonesia by increasing anti-Shia sentiment, and also that returning mujahedin may "bring new life, leadership and ideas to the radical movement at home."[24]

GROWING SECTARIAN STRIFE IN LEBANON

The Syria conflict has allowed Sunni jihadists to experience significant gains in Lebanon, and has produced a tremendous resurgence of sectarian conflict. The major jihadist group that has gained since the conflict began is the Abdullah Azzam Brigades (AAB), named after bin Laden's mentor.

As the U.S. Department of State has explained, AAB's formation was announced in a July 2009 video that claimed credit for a rocket attack against Israel.[25] There are two different branches of AAB. The Lebanese branch is called the Ziad al-Jarrah

Battalions, named after a Lebanese citizen who was one of the 9/11 hijackers, and it has primarily been known for occasional rocket strikes on Israel. Like ISIS, AAB was focused on benefiting from the Syria conflict, and late AAB emir Majid bin Muhammad al-Majid issued guidance regarding what kind of attacks to avoid in Syria in order to win over the population.[26]

AAB had low manpower prior to the onset of the Syrian conflict, with perhaps 150 men in the group's ranks. Its growing capabilities can be seen in recent attacks that it carried out inside Lebanon. The most prominent attack AAB carried out was the November 19, 2013, bombing of the Iranian Embassy in Beirut. This attack is indicative of both AAB's growing capabilities—Iran's Embassy is not an easy target—and also growing sectarianism in Lebanon. AAB also launched a twin suicide attack in Beirut last month that struck an Iranian cultural center.

AAB's attacks come within the context of escalating violence in general, and sectarian violence in particular, inside Lebanon. Some of the early attacks following the onset of anti-Assad protests in Syria struck at U.N. forces, including a May 2011 roadside bomb that struck a U.N. convoy near Sidon, and a July 2011 bomb attack that injured five French U.N. peacekeepers, also near Sidon. U.N. peacekeepers were struck by a roadside bomb for a third time in December 2011, prompting Lebanese Prime Minister Najib Mikati to describe these attacks on peacekeepers as targeting "Lebanon's stability and security."[27]

In addition to these anti-U.N. attacks, occasional violence broke out between anti-Assad protesters and Tripoli's Alawite communities, but clashes became more frequent and more sectarian over time. A variety of incidents demonstrate the progressive growth in sectarian strife:

- The arrest and killing of prominent Lebanese Sunni figures in May 2012 produced instability: after authorities arrested Islamist figure, Shadi al-Mawlawi, resulting street protests descended into violence that killed 10, and the shooting death of Sheikh Ahmad Abdel-Wahad later that month similarly produced rage and unrest.
- In June 2012, after a Lebanese Shia was arrested for firebombing and shooting up the offices of New TV, which was critical of Assad's regime, Shia gunmen erected roadblocks in Beirut, burning tires and firing automatic weapons into the air.[28]
- In July 2012, after a Damascus bombing killed several regime figures close to Assad, celebrations in the Tripoli's Sunni neighborhood Bab al-Tabbeneh descended into clashes with Alawite residents of the Jabal Mohsen neighborhood, leaving one person dead. Clashes between residents of these two neighborhoods have proved to be an enduring feature of how the Syria conflict is being felt in Tripoli.
- In October 2012, a bomb blast in Beirut killed Lebanese intelligence chief Wissam al-Hassan was assassinated, with Syria strongly suspected. This raised immediate concerns about inflaming sectarian tensions, as "black smoke from burning tires ignited by angry men choked the streets of a few neighborhoods in the city" before night fell.[29] Al-Hassan's assassination and the subsequent backlash of violence has had huge repercussions in Lebanon, greatly destabilizing politics and leading to a marked escalation in violence in 2013.

Bombings would further escalate sectarian tensions. On July 9, 2013, a car bomb exploded in Hezbollah-dominated territory in southern Beirut, injuring over 50 people. This attack "increased fears that the spillover from the war in neighboring Syria was entering a dangerous new phase."[30] About a week later, gunmen assassinated Mohammad Darra Jamo, a pro-Assad media commentator, in his Sarafand home.[31] On August 15, 2013, a car bomb struck a Hezbollah stronghold in southern Beirut again, killing 20 and wounding over 100 people. A Sunni Islamist group claimed credit, and promised to continue striking at Hezbollah. On November 19, 2013, AAB carried out its already described bombing of the Iranian Embassy in Beirut. The attack killed at least 22 people, including Iran's cultural attaché, and wounded over 100. On December 4, 2013, high-ranking Hezbollah leader, Hassane Laqees, was assassinated, shot at close range as he parked his car near a south Beirut apartment that he used.[32] On January 2, 2014, another bomb struck a Hezbollah-dominated area in south Beirut, killing at least five and injuring more than 50.

Sunnis were also targeted by bombings. On August 23, 2013, powerful bomb blasts struck two Sunni mosques in Tripoli whose imams had ties to Syrian rebels (the Al-Taqwa and Al-Salam mosques), killing at least 42 and wounding about 600. The level of carnage in these attacks hadn't been seen in Lebanon since the 1980s. On December 27, 2013, former Lebanese Finance Minister and U.S. Ambassador Mohamad Chatah (a member of the Sunni community) was killed by a car bomb.

Chatah's vocal opposition to Hezbollah and the Assad regime made the list of possible perpetrators rather clear.

Lebanon-based Alawites have also been the victims of sectarian violence. On February 20, 2014, an official in the pro-Assad Arab Democratic Party (ADP), Abdel-Rahman Diab was shot and killed by masked gunmen on a motorcycle while driving on the coastal Mina highway. As news of his killing spread, ADP fighters in the hotspot Jabal Mohsen neighborhood "began sniping at their rival neighborhoods of Mallouleh and Mankoubin." [33]

The sectarian strife in Lebanon is particularly intense, but the Syria war has also magnified sectarianism throughout the region, and beyond. As researchers Aaron Y. Zelin and Phillip Smyth demonstrate, the way this conflict has lined up—with Sunni salafists battling Alawites and Iranian-backed Shias—has caused dehumanizing sectarian language to become a more common part of discourse.[34] Zelin and Smyth note that "many players are pursuing a long-term dehumanization strategy because they view this as an existential cosmic religious battle between salafi Sunnism and Khomeinist Shiism." In turn, there have been sectarian incidents not only in the region, but in countries further from the main battlefield, such as Australia, Azerbaijan, Britain, and Egypt.

As for Lebanon, the spillover of the Syrian conflict can be seen on three levels. The first is the increase in sectarianism that has blossomed into violence within Lebanon, as I have detailed at some length. Second, there is the increase in conflict between Syria and Lebanon: Syria has carried out cross-border attacks against rebel targets in Lebanon. Third, the growing presence of refugees from Syria is putting an increasing strain on the Lebanese economy and society.

RESURGENT JIHADISM IN IRAQ

At the time of the U.S. troop withdrawal from Iraq in December 2011, ISIS, which is the successor to Al-Qaeda in Iraq (AQI), "was still able to conduct attacks, but the organization was isolated, disrupted, and did not pose an existential threat to the state," as demonstrated by the fact that, "from September 2010 to December 2011, monthly fatalities in Iraq stabilized in the 300–400 range." [35] The group has experienced a dramatic renewal since then: in 2013, more than 7,800 civilians lost their lives in violent attacks, while ISIS was able to launch a stunning offensive that captured large portions of Fallujah and Ramadi in January 2014.

Factors other than Syria also played a role in ISIS's rebound, but the Syria war has also helped bring new life to the jihadist group due to the already explained popularity and legitimacy that the Syria jihad enjoys. When the Syria conflict escalated, ISIS already had an existing infrastructure that gave it one of the best ground games among rebel factions, and which helped the group gain territory and prestige. In turn, it also attracted additional resources and more recruits. The symbiotic relationship between the Syria conflict and ISIS's resurgence in Iraq is further illustrated by administration officials' belief that "most" suicide bombers striking inside Iraq during a recent surge in the tactic's use "are coming in from Syria." [36]

The Syria conflict has strengthened ISIS in four major ways. First, ISIS experienced a surge in popularity by being at the forefront of a popular jihad, though its brutal tactics could undercut this gain. Second, the abundance of people willing to fight the Assad regime provided the group with an easy source of recruits. Today, ISIS is estimated to have around 7,000 fighters in its ranks.[37] Third, the conflict made funding easier to obtain, both from external financiers and also through extorting "tax" revenues from citizens and militarily capturing industries in Syria. (As will be discussed subsequently, ISIS's recent expulsion from al-Qaeda likely diminishes its external sources of funding.) And a fourth factor contributing to ISIS's gains has been its ability to control territory in Syria and otherwise operate from the Syrian side of the border. Iraqi Deputy Interior Minister, Adnan al-Asadi, has explained that ISIS "is deployed in vast desert areas on both sides of the Iraqi-Syrian borders that are difficult for any army to control," which makes Iraq's fight against ISIS "require a lot of time and resources." [38]

One of ISIS's striking achievements last year was the July 2013 prison break from the notorious high-security Abu Ghraib prison outside of Baghdad. The tactics it employed included suicide and car bombs, an attack against another prison in Taji as a diversion, and inside assistance from some of the personnel charged with guarding the prison.[39] An Iraqi security official told Reuters that the attack was "obviously a terrorist attack" designed to "free convicted terrorists with al-Qaeda." [40] The most commonly cited figure for the number of prisoners who managed to escape is 500, and there was a particularly high concentration of important ISIS leaders and operatives in this group. Given the manner in which prison breaks and prisoner releases have bolstered the jihadist movement in the past, the Abu Ghraib incident is likely to magnify the challenges that Iraq faces.

One issue of immediate relevance regarding the future of ISIS, al-Qaeda, and the Syria jihad is ISIS's expulsion from the al-Qaeda network on February 2, 2014, when al-Qaeda's senior leadership announced it was no longer affiliated with ISIS. This separation was a long time coming. ISIS had been fighting with other Syrian rebel factions, and al-Qaeda's senior leadership ordered it to submit to mediation to resolve these tensions. ISIS paid lip service to these demands but in practice flouted the mediation orders. Though there was a great deal of behind-the-scenes maneuvering between the two, ultimately al-Qaeda issued a statement announcing that ISIS was no longer part of the organization.

There was an immediate escalation in tensions in Syria following ISIS's expulsion from AQ. After other rebel factions increasingly targeted ISIS, it has largely retreated to its northern Syria stronghold of Raqqa, which it believes to be the most defensible position during a difficult and uncertain time. There will also be implications for the shape of jihadism beyond the region. ISIS had been in open defiance of al-Qaeda's senior leadership (AQSL) until it was finally expelled from the organization. If it prospers despite defying al-Qaeda's leadership, does that weaken AQSL's ability to have influence over other affiliates? Might AQ financiers and potential recruits throw their weight behind competing jihadist sources of power? There are some signs of the strains being placed on the al-Qaeda network by this separation. Jihadist forums now feature users openly siding with ISIS, and condemning al-Qaeda's recognized branches in Syria. Further, jihadist groups affiliated with al-Qaeda are deeply divided over how to address the split between ISIS and al-Qaeda.

The stakes involved in this question were raised significantly at the end of February when Abu Khalid al-Suri, a longtime leader within al-Qaeda and one of the founding members of the Syrian rebel group Ahrar al-Sham, was killed by a suicide bomber, with ISIS being blamed by many jihadists, including by Ahrar al-Sham.[41]

Though the fragmentation of al-Qaeda is one possible outcome of the ISIS–AQ split, some public sphere analysis has gotten ahead of the facts in this regard. ISIS itself risks weakness and fragmentation. Major clerics like Abdallah Muhammad al-Muhaysini have called for ISIS fighters to defect to other jihadist factions.[42] ISIS's retreat to Raqqa—abandoning such sources of income as Deir al-Zour's grain mills and factories in the process—is indicative of its feelings of vulnerability in Syria. And ISIS has seen new competitors emerge even inside Iraq. In late February, a new jihadist group called Al-Murabitin Front in Iraq announced its formation, something that many online jihadists believe to be a new al-Qaeda branch designed to counter ISIS's influence.[43] Al-Murabitin has already claimed its first attacks in Iraq, posting statements to the Hanin jihadist web forum claiming bomb attacks against Iraqi military vehicles.[44]

The ISIS–AQ split is an important inflection point that may have an enormous impact on jihadism within Syria and beyond. The ramifications warrant close attention.

CONCLUSION

The Syria war is already a major tragedy. It is likely to have a tragic ending, too, and the U.S. is probably unable to avert that even if it chooses to become far more deeply involved in the country's civil war.

At a policymaking level, the U.S.'s response to developments in Syria can best be described as confused. We haven't defined our desired end state: we seem to vaguely know what we don't want to happen, but have little or no idea how to get there. Nor have we defined the kind of means we are willing to devote in pursuit of whatever goals we think are in our strategic interest. What do we want? What are we prepared to do to achieve it?

It is also important to bear in mind that the more involved we choose to be, the greater the danger that the U.S. will be further drawn into the conflict in ways that we do not intend. I believe that the U.S. should choose a course of limited engagement for several reasons:

- The U.S.'s strategic interests in Syria that it can realistically achieve are relatively low.
- It is obvious that the U.S. doesn't understand the players on the ground well, and so will have great difficulty selecting a desirable set of players to back.
- Indeed, it is highly likely that U.S. aid to rebel factions will fall into jihadist hands.
- There are cognizable risks of the U.S. being drawn into the Syria quagmire beyond what it intends.

Let us not sugarcoat what a strategy of limited engagement means. I have noted that it's possible the Assad regime could collapse faster than anticipate; but if the U.S. chooses a strategy of limited engagement, we have to be prepared for the converse possibility, that Assad may crush the rebels. It comes down to a question of tradeoffs, and the fact that there are costs to any option the U.S. might choose.

A strategy of limited engagement is not the same as a strategy of nonengagement. A limited-engagement strategy would recognize that the U.S. is probably incapable of truly addressing Syria's problems—certainly not at an acceptable cost—and so our overarching priority is containing the spillover. One priority for this strategy should be ameliorating the humanitarian crisis that the Syrian war has created, focusing efforts on refugees from Syria. There are both strong moral and humanitarian reasons for doing so, but also strategic reasons: the potential for radicalization within the refugee problem is a real concern.

It is at the very least acceptable, and perhaps desirable, for the U.S. to provide small arms to rebel factions. The harm in doing so is relatively small if these arms fall into the wrong hands, given the large amount of light weaponry that is already in Syria; and the U.S. can derive specific benefits from providing light arms to rebels. Those benefits should not involve trying to lengthen or draw out the conflict; but, if the policy is implemented right, it can provide the U.S. with both a presence and platform. The U.S. might use this position to gather intelligence and better map the rebel factions; and it may be able to gain some degree of influence over the rebels, although the potential for gaining influence should not be overstated.

There have been suggestions that the U.S. should send antitank or antiaircraft weapons to Syrian rebels. Such a course presents significant risks that the weaponry would end up in jihadist hands, or the hands of others who would wish harm to the United States or its allies. For this reason, under the approach I suggest the U.S. should refuse to escalate by providing this more advanced weaponry, unless (a) a clear and specific strategic interest can be advanced by the provision of imagery, and (b) the U.S. can ensure to its satisfaction that the weapons will not end up in jihadist hands. At present, neither of these conditions exist.

One of the fundamental dilemmas the U.S. must confront in the 21st century security environment is the reality of severely constrained resources. The U.S. no longer has the luxury of living in the unipolar world that existed a dozen years ago. Not only is the U.S. now incapable of responding with full vigor to every perceived threat—doing so would ensure that we lack the resources to advance our most pressing interests—but we will also be increasingly challenged, including by those we regard as our allies.

Just as we no longer have the luxury of living in a unipolar world, we also no longer have the luxury of being able to muddle through with poor foreign-policy strategy and expect that there will be no costs. This means that we will have to carefully consider what kind of resources and commitments we are willing to make in advance of any potential commitment. When the U.S. drew a redline over Syrian chemical weapons use that it was apparently unable to enforce, that resulted in real damage to other countries' perception of what U.S. security guarantees mean.

One sad reality of the 21st century is that lives will often be lost in other parts of the world, and we won't be able to do anything about it. This should give us no comfort, but we must be realistic. The course to maintaining American power in the 21st century begins with conserving our resources, and in Syria achieving real strategic gains at an acceptable cost will be difficult.

Thank you again for inviting me to testify today. I look forward to answering your questions.

Notes

[1] This testimony focuses on Sunni foreign fighters because they will have a profound impact on the future shape of the jihadist movement. However, the conflict has also attracted Shia foreign fighters to the battlefield, as well as other nonstate actors who chose to enter the battle on Syrian President Bashar al-Assad's side. For some of the best work on this subject, it is worth following Phillip Smyth's excellent feature "Hizballah Cavalcade" at the website Jihadology (www.jihadology.net). As of the writing of this testimony, the last foreign fighters in Syria to attract major media attention were fighting on Assad's side: They were a couple of L.A. gang members who swore they would fight Assad's "enemigos." One of the men, identifying himself as "Creeper from the G'd up 13 Gang," explained his role in Syria: "I'm gangbanging, homie." Middle East Media Research Institute, video clip #4170, March 1, 2014.

[2] Aaron Zelin et al., "Up to 11,00 Foreign Fighters in Syria; Steep Rise Among Western Europeans," ICSR Insight, December 17, 2013.

[3] Adam Entous & Siobhan Gorman, "Behind Assad's Comeback, A Mismatch in Commitments," Wall Street Journal, December 31, 2013 (noting that "the civil war could last another decade or more, based on a Central Intelligence Agency analysis of the history of insurgencies that recently departed Deputy Director Michael Morell privately shared with lawmakers").

[4] Emile Hokayem, "Syria's Uprising and the Fracturing of the Levant Kindle" ed. (London: International Institute for Strategic Studies, 2013), loc. 161 of 3617.

[5] See discussion of fragmented sovereignty in Klejda Mulaj, "Violent Non-State Actors: Exploring Their State Relations, Legitimation, and Operationality," in Klejda Mulaj ed., Violent Non-State Actors in World Politics (New York: Columbia University Press, 2010), pp. 7–10.

[6] Joseph Holliday, "The Struggle for Syria in 2011: An Operational and Regional Analysis" (Washington, DC: Institute for the Study of War, 2011), p. 13.

[7] Hokayem, "Syria's Uprising," loc. 1219 of 3617.

[8] Tony Badran, "How Assad Stayed in Power—And How He'll Try to Keep It," Foreign Affairs, December 1, 2011.

[9] "Assad Fails to Break Syrian Stalemate Despite Rebel Infighting," Financial Times, Jan. 16, 2014.

[10] For information on Russia's naval base, see Christopher Harmer, "Backgrounder: Naval Base Tartus," Institute for the Study of War, July 31, 2012.

[11] Phil Sands, Justin Vela & Suha Maayeh, "Assad Regime Set Free Extremists from Prison to Fire Up Trouble During Peaceful Uprising," The National (U.A.E.), Jan. 21, 2014; Ruth Sherlock, "Syria's Assad Accused of Boosting al-Qaeda with Secret Oil Deals," Telegraph (U.K.), Jan. 20, 2014.

[12] Serkan Demirtas, "Ankara: Assad Leaves Turkish Border to Kurds," Hürriyet Daily News, July 25, 2012.

[13] Nicholas Blanford, "What Syrian Rebel Infighting Means for Assad," Christian Science Monitor, Jan. 13, 2014.

[14] Mohammed M. Hafez, "Jihad after Iraq: Lessons from the Arab Afghans Phenomenon," CTC Sentinel (Combating Terrorism Center at West Point), Mar. 2008.

[15] Indictment, United States v. Arnaout, 02 CR 892 (N.D. Ill., 2002), p. 2; 9/11 Commission Report: "Final Report of the National Commission on Terrorist Attacks Upon the United States" (New York: W. W. Norton, 2004), p. 56.

[16] Tareekh Osama memorandum, 1988, introduced by prosecution at Benevolence International Foundation trial, Northern District of Illinois, 2002–2003.

[17] Zelin et al., "Up to 11,00 Foreign Fighters in Syria."

[18] Thomas Hegghammer, " 'Should I Stay or Should I Go': Explaining Variation in Western Jihadists' Choice between Domestic and Foreign Fighting," American Political Science Review, Feb. 2013, p. 10.

[19] Zelin et al., "Up to 11,00 Foreign Fighters in Syria."

[20] Rana al-Sabbagh, "Jordan Faces Growing Salafi-Jihadist Threat," Al-Monitor, Feb. 4, 2014.

[21] Taimur Khan, "Prince Mohammed Appointment Highlights Saudi Arabia's Terrorism Concerns Over Syria," The National (U.A.E.), Feb. 25, 2014.

[22] Michael Winter, "Report: Saudis Sent Death-Row Inmates to Fight Syria," USA Today, Jan. 21, 2013.

[23] "Indonesians and the Syria Conflict," Institute for Policy Analysis of Conflict Report No. 6, Jan. 30, 2014, p. 1.

[24] Ibid., p. 10.

[25] U.S. Department of State, "Foreign Terrorist Organizations," May 30, 2013.

[26] Bill Roggio, "Abdullah Azzam Brigades Names Leader, Advises Against Attacks in Syria's Cities," Long War Journal, June 27, 2012.

[27] Anthony Shadid, "U.N. Peacekeepers Wounded in Southern Lebanon Attack," New York Times, Dec. 12, 2011.

[28] Rob Nordland, "Assad Supporters Suspected in New Beirut Incidents," New York Times, June 26, 2012.

[29] Anne Barnard, "Blast in Beirut is Seen as an Extension of Syria's War," New York Times, Oct. 19, 2012.

[30] Anne Barnard, "Car Bombing Injures Dozens in Hezbollah Section of Beirut," New York Times, July 9, 2013.

[31] Oliver Holmes, "Gunmen Kill Pro-Assad Figure in Lebanon as Syria War Spreads," Reuters, July 17, 2013.

[32] Anne Barnard, "Major Hezbollah Figure, Tied to Syrian War, is Assassinated Near Beirut," New York Times, Dec. 4, 2013.

[33] Misbah al-Ali, "Pro-Assad Party Issues Ultimatum Over Official's Killing," Daily Star (Lebanon), Feb. 20, 2014.

[34] Aaron Y. Zelin & Phillip Smyth, "The Vocabulary of Sectarianism," Foreign Policy, Jan. 29, 2014.

[35] Jessica D. Lewis, "Al-Qaeda in Iraq Resurgent" (Washington, DC: Institute for the Study of War, Sept. 2013), p. 9.

[36] Senior administration official, U.S. Department of State, "Background Briefing on U.S.-Iraq Political and Diplomatic JCC Meeting and the U.S.-Iraq Bilateral Relationship Under the Strategic Framework Agreement," Aug. 15, 2013.

[37] "What ISIS, an Al-Qaeda Affiliate in Syria, Really Wants," The Economist Jan. 20, 2014.

[38] Harith Hasan, "ISIS Exploits Weak Iraqi, Syrian States," Al-Monitor, Nov. 29, 2013.

[39] Adam Schreck & Qassim Abdul-Zahra, "Abu Ghraib Prison Break: Hundreds Of Detainees, Including Senior Al-Qaeda Members, Escape Facility," Associated Press, July 22, 2013.

[40] Kareem Raheem & Ziad Al-Sinjary, "Al-Qaeda Militants Flee Iraq Jail in Violent Mass Break-Out," Reuters, July 22, 2013.

[41] Maria Abi-Habib, "Al-Qaeda Emissary in Syria Killed by Rival Islamist Rebels," Wall Street Journal, February 23, 2014

[42] Thomas Joscelyn, "Pro-Al-Qaeda Saudi Cleric Calls for ISIS Members to Defect," Long War Journal, February 3, 2014.

[43] BBC Monitoring in English, Feb. 26, 2014.

[44] BBC Monitoring in English, Feb. 28, 2014.

The CHAIRMAN. Dr. Levitt.

STATEMENT OF MATTHEW LEVITT, PH.D., DIRECTOR FOR STEIN PROGRAM ON COUNTERTERRORISM AND INTELLIGENCE, THE WASHINGTON INSTITUTE FOR NEAR EAST POLICY, WASHINGTON, DC

Dr. LEVITT. Thank you very much, Chairman Menendez, Ranking Member Corker, members of the committee. It is an honor to be here to testify before you today. There is of course the multiple connections between the two issues of Ukraine and Syria, not the least is that President Assad just announced that he is supporting Putin in that conflict.

The war in Syria is a humanitarian catastrophe that threatens to tear the region apart along sectarian lines. It has injected new oxygen into terrorist groups and movements driven by violent ideologies around the region, including but by no means limited to groups formerly associated with al-Qaeda. In fact, we are now facing a sharp rise in violent extremism within both the radical Sunni and the Shiite camps.

Over the past few weeks, much of the discussion on Syria has focused on diplomatic talks and potential threats to the West, but this hearing is about the regional implications of Syria and so I want to focus on three things. The first is the flow of foreign fighters to Syria from across the Middle East and then back home and the impact this is already having in the region, not just their potential to go to Europe or here, a very real threat, but in the region, which is already happening.

Second, the especially pernicious sectarian nature of the conflict in hand; and third, the very sharp increase as a result of the war in dangerous macrotrends, the kinds of things that create conditions that are conducive to long-term violence and instability in the region.

As I was thinking about this hearing, I reread a declassified 1993 report written by the State Department's INR, Intelligence and Research Branch, in which they discuss things like the foreign fighters coming home from Afghanistan. If you take ''Afghanistan'' and insert ''Syria,'' if you take out things that are clear to 1993 and clear to today, this report could have been written yesterday. Consider how then and now, as Daveed said, fighters are traveling from around the world to go fight on either side of this increasingly sectarian war. Then note that the greatest number of foreign fighters on both sides have come from the Middle East.

The likelihood, and we are already seeing it, is that the majority of radicalized fighters are going to go home and attack their homes in the region before they come and strike in Europe or in the United States. We have already seen an Israeli Arab convicted for going to fight with Jibhat al-Nusra in Israel. We have already seen cases of suicide bombers who were going to go to fight in Syria and in the end were sent instead to Tunisia. We have seen people coming back from Syria and carrying out attacks in Egypt. We see a fully Moroccan jihadist organization created in Syria, and the cases go on and on.

But none of it should surprise. Twenty-one years ago INR noted that the support network that funneled money, supplies, and manpower to supplant the then-Afghan mujahedin was now contributing experienced fighters to militant Islamic groups worldwide, and it will be again today. As one point of that 1993 report is entitled, "When the Boys Come Home."

Consider the role of Libya then at the time and then think about today Libya's Ansar al-Sharia operating on the ground, not in Libya but in Syria, in Latakia, for example, setting up a bakery and organizing an Ansar al-Sharia branded aid for Sunni communities.

Meanwhile, how complicated has it got? You have Iran not only supporting Assad, not only supporting Hezbollah, but also supporting al-Qaeda elements moving foreign fighters and raising money, in particular from Kuwait, through Iran and knowingly allowing al-Qaeda elements to do so within Iran.

In terms of the proxy issues, this is no longer a simple rebellion. This has grown into a classic case of a proxy war between Sunnis, Sunni Gulf States, and Iran on the other. The sectarian vocabulary that is used to dehumanize the other is something that is going to set the stage for the next decade.

The bottom line is that, while the war itself might at some level be negotiable, maybe, the sectarianism is not and is almost certainly going to create conditions for instability over the next decade.

Finally, a last comment on the trending toward instability. The NIC, the National Intelligence Council, had a great study called "Global Trends 2030, Alternative Worlds." It talks there about things that it describes as "looming disequilibria." Every one of those things we are seeing today, problems with education, health, poverty, forced migration, humanitarian assistance needs, the economic impact on fragile economies in the neighborhood, Jordan in particular, Lebanon in particular. This is something we are seeing in spades now.

When the NIC published its report, it actually anticipated that this kind of chronic instability in the Middle East was something we would see. They highlighted Iraq, Libya, Yemen, and Syria as places where we could see things like this, Bahrain. But clearly there is no way they could have anticipated what we are seeing today.

I submit that the United States is not doing anywhere near enough to address these critical problems, and failure to respond effectively to this crisis has led in part to the increasing horrific consequences today. Even if we do not want either camp to win tomorrow because there are bad guys on both sides, there are certain things we have to do. We must degrade the regime and the extremist capabilities to create conditions for moderates' victory some time tomorrow.

Also, we have to mitigate the regime and the extremists' ability to continue to do damage today. Simply doing humanitarian aid is addressing the symptoms. What are we doing to stop the foreign fighters? What are we doing to stop the barrel bombs so that more humanitarian crises are not created tomorrow?

If I can put it in one last concluding statement, it is this: Las Vegas rules do not apply in Syria. I applaud the committee for holding this hearing today specifically on the spillover effects in the region because what happens in Syria will not remain in Syria.

[The prepared statement of Dr. Levitt follows:]

PREPARED STATEMENT OF DR. MATTHEW LEVITT [1]

Chairman Menendez, Ranking Member Corker, members of the committee, thank you for the opportunity to testify before you today about such a critical and timely issue.

The war in Syria is a humanitarian catastrophe. It threatens to tear the region apart along sectarian lines. It has injected new oxygen into groups and movements driven by violent Islamist ideologies, including but by no means limited to groups formally associated with al-Qaeda. Indeed, we are now faced with a sharp rise in violent extremism from within both the radical Sunni and Shiite camps.

Over the past few weeks, much of the discussion related to the war in Syria has focused on either diplomatic talks in Switzerland (which appear to be going nowhere fast) or the potential threats to the West in general and the U.S. homeland in particular posed by the Syrian jihad. These are critical issues, to be sure, but I am very pleased that this committee is holding today's hearing on the regional implications of the war in Syria.

As Director of National Intelligence James Clapper recently noted, we can expect an increase in political uncertainty and violence across the region in 2014.[2] There are many reasons this will be the case, not all of which are directly tied to the war in Syria. For today's purposes, however, I would like to address three types of fallout from the war in Syria that are certain to cause significant spillover of one kind or another: First, the flow of foreign fighters to Syria from across the Middle East and the impact this is certain to have on regional stability; second, the especially pernicious sectarian nature of the conflict at hand, and the impact that will have on Lebanon in particular; and third, the sharp increase—as a result of the war—in dangerous macrotrends, from refugees and population displacement to poverty, hunger, and lack of adequate health care, that create conditions conducive to violence and instability.

"WHEN THE BOYS COME HOME"

Fifteen years from now, when classified documents produced today begin to be declassified, we will surely look back with some discomfort at just how far off some of our judgments were when written in 2014. Such is the nature of intelligence assessments. I worry, however, that we may look back 15 years hence and find ourselves dealing with a laundry list of difficult problems that are in large part the result of actions taken, or not taken, today.

This reflection is underscored by rereading a declassified August 1993 report, "The Wandering Mujahidin: Armed and Dangerous," written by the State Department's Bureau of Intelligence and Research (INR).[3] Its subject was the possible spillover effect of Afghan mujahedin fighters and support networks moving on to fight in other jihad conflicts, alongside other militant Islamic groups worldwide. Much of the report could be applied as equally to the themes we find ourselves facing today as it did when it was written 21 years ago.

Consider how fighters are traveling from around the world to go fight on either side of the increasingly sectarian war in Syria. Much of the discussion about foreign fighters traveling to Syria has focused on radicalized Muslim youth coming from Western countries—Europe, North America, Australia—which presents an especially disconcerting threat to homeland security given that these Western passport holders are likely to return home far more radicalized than when they left. These individuals are also more often than not fighting with groups like Jabhat al-Nusra (JN) or the Islamic State of Iraq and al-Sham (ISIS), at least some of which, DNI Clapper recently testified, aspire to attack the United States.[4] But the greatest numbers of foreign fighters, on both the Sunni and Shiite sides of the equation, have come from the Middle East. Indeed, it must be noted that while most people focus on the Sunni foreign fighter phenomenon, there are at least as many Shiite foreign fighters in Syria today. Most are from Iraq, but others have come from as far afield as Yemen, Afghanistan, and even Australia.

Earlier this month DNI Clapper estimated that more than 7,000 fighters have traveled to Syria from more than 50 countries.[5] In an independent study in December, my colleague, Aaron Zelin, estimated the numbers to be some 8,500 foreign fighters from 74 different countries. His estimates of the range of foreign fighters from across the region who have come to fight on the Sunni side of the war in Syria are equally telling:[6]

ARAB WORLD

Country	Low	High	Country	Low	High
Kuwait	54	71	Lebanon	65	890
Tunisia	379	970	Jordan	175	2,089
Libya	330	556	Iraq	59	97
Algeria	68	123	Egypt	118	358
Palestine	73	114	Saudi Arabia	380	1,010
Sudan	2	96	Yemen	13	110
Morocco	76	91	United Arab Emirates	13	13
Mauritania	2	2	Qatar	14	14
Bahrain	12	12	Oman	1	1

On the Shiite side of the equation, Lebanese Hezbollah and Iraqi Shiite militants from groups like Asaib Ahl al-Haqq and Kataib Hezbollah make up a majority of the Shiites fighting in support of the Bashar al-Assad regime. Some estimate that as many as 5,000 Lebanese Hezbollah have been active in Syria, on a rotational basis.[7] Iraqi Shiites fighting in Syria are also estimated to be as high as 5,000.[8] And Iranians are present in smaller support and advising roles. In April 2011, the entire Quds Force of Iran's Islamic Revolutionary Guard Corps (IRGC) was designated by President Obama's Executive Order 13572 for human rights violations in Syria.[9] Iran's Ministry of Intelligence and Security (MOIS) forces as well as its Law Enforcement Forces (LEF) have also been active in Syria, and have likewise been designated by the U.S. Treasury Department for human rights abuses.[10] Shiites from Saudi Arabia, Cote d'Ivoire, and Afghanistan have also flown to Syria to fight on behalf of the regime, and Yemeni Houthi fighters are reported to be going to Syria through Hezbollah camps in Lebanon to fight with the regime and Hezbollah.[11]

In Syria, these foreign fighters are learning new and more dangerous tools of the trade in a very hands-on way, and those who do not die on the battlefield will ultimately disperse to all corners of the world better trained and still more radicalized than they were before. DNI Clapper stressed that it is not only foreign fighters who are drawn to Syria today but also ''technologies and techniques that pose particular problems to our defenses.''[12]

''We are concerned,'' CIA Director John Brennan testified, ''about the use of Syrian territory by the al-Qaeda organization to recruit individuals . . . to use Syria as a launching pad'' for attacks on the West.[13] But the threat is not limited to actual al-Qaeda groups or operatives, nor is it limited to attacks targeting the West. The majority of radicalized fighters are likely to return home and attack their own homelands even before they seek to strike ours, in large part because the events that have followed the Arab Spring have created conditions favorable for militant Islamist revival—social and militant both—across the region.

Consider just a few regional reverberations of the Syrian jihad already being felt today:

- This week an Israeli court convicted an Israeli Arab citizen of joining Jabhat al-Nusra. The presiding judge expressed concern over the danger posed by Israeli citizens who join the war in Syria and return home, where ''they could use the military training and ideological indoctrination acquired in Syria to commit terror attacks, indoctrinate others or gather intelligence for use in attacks by anti-Israel organizations.''[14]
- For many in the region and beyond, going to fight in Syria is a natural and unremarkable decision. For these people, the fight in Syria is a defensive jihad to protect fellow Sunni Muslims—women and children—from the Assad regime's indiscriminate attacks on civilian population centers. And so it is that Ahmed Abdullah al-Shaya, the poster boy for Saudi Arabia's deradicalization program—which boasts a tiny 1.5 percent recidivism rate from among its 2,400 graduates—has now turned up on the battlefield in Syria.[15]
- ''Tunisia's revolution and those in Syria, Egypt and Yemen, and Libya gave us a chance to set up an Islamic state and sharia law, and in the Maghreb first,'' explained a young Tunisian Salafist in Tunis, Abu Salah. ''We want nothing less than an Islamic state in Tunisia, and across the region. The first step must be Syria. I am proud of our brothers in Syria, and I will go there myself in a few weeks.''[16]
- Another young Tunisian, Ayman Saadi, who was raised in a middle-class family with a secular tradition, was stopped from going to fight in Syria several times by his parents before he finally snuck out of the country to Benghazi. He

trained there for a short time, but instead of going on to Syria, he was instructed to go back to Tunisia to carry out a suicide attack at a Presidential mausoleum; Saadi was tackled by guards before he could trigger his explosives. Just before that, another bomber managed to kill only himself at a nearby beach resort popular with foreign tourists.[17]

- In Egypt, the government is already facing high levels of violence largely in reaction to the deposition of former President Muhammad Morsi. Incidents of militants returning from Syria, too, and carrying out violent acts against the government have occurred. The Sinai militant group Ansar Beit al-Maqdis attracts many returnees and has claimed responsibility for a number of attacks in recent months. In September, Walid Badr, a former Egyptian Army officer, after returning from Syria conducted a suicide attack that narrowly missed Egyptian Interior Minister Muhammad Ibrahim, instead injuring 19 others.[18] In November, Ansar Beit al-Maqdis published a propaganda video featuring a segment of a speech by the late Abu Omar al-Baghdadi, the former head of al-Qaeda's Islamic State in Iraq (ISI), which later evolved into ISIS.''[19]

- In August, a new, fully Moroccan jihadist organization called Harakat Sham al-Islam was created in Syria. The group reportedly aims not only to recruit fighters for the Syrian war but also to establish a jihadist organization within Morocco itself: ''Although the [group's] name refers to Syria and its theater is Syria, the majority of group members are Moroccans. The group's creation was also announced in the Rif Latakia, where most Moroccan jihadists who go to Syria are based.''[20]

- Last month, an Iraqi newspaper ceased publishing after receiving death threats from the Iranian-backed Shiite militia Asaib Ahl al-Haqq. Two bombs were placed in its office in Baghdad, and protestors carrying photographs of Asaib Ahl al-Haqq's leader demanded the paper be shut down. Members openly admit to ''ramp[ing] up targeted killings.''[21] The militia has been active in Iraq since the American-led war, in which it carried out thousands of attacks on U.S. soldiers, and currently has forces in Syria.[22]

- Last week Jordanian border guards foiled an attempt to smuggle a large amount of ammunition and other material not from Jordan into Syria, but from Syria in Jordan.[23]

None of this should surprise. Twenty-one years ago, INR reported that ''the support network that funneled money, supplies, and manpower to supplement the Afghan Mujahidin is now contributing experienced fighters to militant Islamic groups worldwide.'' When these veteran fighters dispersed, the report presciently predicted, ''their knowledge of communications equipment and experiences in logistics planning will enhance the organizational and offensive capabilities of the militant groups to which they are returning.'' A section of the 1993 report, entitled ''When the Boys Come Home,'' noted that these veteran volunteer fighters ''are welcomed as victorious Muslim fighters of a successful jihad against a superpower'' and ''have won the respect of many Muslims—Arab and non-Arab—who venerate the jihad.''

At that time, these mujahedin returned to Yemen, Egypt, Sudan, Algeria, Libya, and beyond, where they trained local militants and further radicalized local groups. Libya, the 1993 report noted, was once one of the largest backers of Afghan warlord Gulbuddin Hekmatyar (since then designated a terrorist by the United States and the United Nations)[24] but ''now fears the returning veterans and has lashed out publicly against them.''[25] Indeed, several of these Libyan veterans formed the Libyan Islamic Fighting Group (LIFG) and became senior members of core al-Qaeda. In 2006, the U.S. Government would note that ''The Libyan Islamic Fighting Group threatens global safety and stability through the use of violence and its ideological alliance with al-Qaeda and other brutal terrorist organizations.''[26] Today, Libya's Ansar al-Sharia is operating on the ground in Syria. In Latakia, the group has set up a bakery and is organizing Ansar al-Sharia-branded aid for Sunni communities.[27]

But it is not just al-Qaeda-affiliated groups that are active in Syria. As the Treasury Department recently revealed, elements of the al-Qaeda core remain active and involved in the Syrian jihad. On February 6, the Treasury Department designated Iran-based Islamic Jihad Union facilitator Olimzhon Adkhamovich Sadikov (also known as Jafar al-Uzbeki and Jafar Muidinov) for providing logistical support and funding to al-Qaeda's Iran-based network. An associate of Yasin al-Suri, a previously designated al-Qaeda leader in Iran, Sadikov serves as a Mashhad-based smuggler helping extremists and operatives to transit Iran in and out of Pakistan and Afghanistan. The Iran-based al-Qaeda network also helps operatives and terrorist leaders travel from Pakistan to Syria via Turkey, and facilitates the transfer of funds from gulf-based donors—including ''an extensive network of Kuwaiti jihadist donors''—to al-Qaeda core and other affiliated elements, including Jabhat al-Nusra in Syria. This Iran-based network, the Treasury Department noted, ''operates there with the knowledge of Iranian authorities,'' indicating that Iran is not only supporting Hezbollah and the Assad regime but also fanning the flames of sectarian violence by knowingly allowing al-Qaeda to support its elements in Syria from Iranian territory.[28]

And yet there are also signs that al-Qaeda core elements may be concerned that the Syrian jihad could leave them on the sidelines and undermine their relevance. Events in Syria are quickly changing the nature of the jihadist enterprise. Its epicenter is no longer Afghanistan, Pakistan, Iraq, or Yemen, but the heart of the Levant—al-Sham—in Syria. There, both ISIS and Jabhat al-Nusra are fighting the Assad regime and its Shiite allies and more moderate Syrian rebels. The two groups have not merged, and only one (al-Nusra) has pledged allegiance to Ayman al-Zawahiri. Indeed, when Zawahiri instructed ISIS to focus on Iraq and leave the Syrian theater to al-Nusra, ISIS leader Abu Bakr al-Baghdadi flatly refused. This month, Zawahiri responded in kind, blaming ISIS for ''the enormity of the disaster that afflicted the Jihad in Syria'' and disavowing its ties to al-Qaeda. ''ISIS,'' Zawahiri insisted, ''is not a branch of al-Qaeda and we have no organizational relationship with it.''[29]

Meanwhile, other Islamist groups, such as Ahrar al-Sham, remain independent even as they share some ideological underpinnings with al-Qaeda. Today, the jihadist centers that are drawing new recruits, donations, and foreign fighters are not exclusive to al-Qaeda. Knowing that, Zawahiri perhaps felt the need to be able to claim something big that jihadist fighters of all shapes and sizes could rally around. What better than an attack on Israel? And so, on January 22, Israeli officials announced that, several weeks before, they had disrupted what they described as an ''advanced'' al-Qaeda terrorist plot in Israel. Although al-Qaeda-inspired jihadists had targeted Israel before (three men who had plotted an attack near Hebron were killed in a shootout with police in November), this marked the first time that senior al-Qaeda leaders were directly involved in such plans.[30]

The extent to which the Syrian jihad is driven by al-Qaeda core, its affiliates, or other violent Islamist groups is a matter of debate, but it is clear that there is no more of a single command center today than there was 21 years ago. The 1993 report describes several trends that remain issues of serious concern, including some of the same streams of financial support that continue to finance today's militant Islamist groups (though not all—fundraising for the Syrian jihad through social media is now a significant issue). To the present-day reader, who will digest this 1993 report with an eye toward the conflict in Syria, perhaps the most disturbing analytical judgment—which could have been pulled out of a current National Intelligence Estimate—is this:

> The war-era network of state sponsors and private patrons which continues to support the mujahidin has no rigid structure and no clearly defined command center, but receives guidance from several popular Islamic leaders and financial support from charitable Islamic organizations and wealthy individuals. Key figures who have emerged as the mentors of the mujahidin provide one another with the contacts and conduits needed to keep the militant groups they support in business.

The network circa 1993 was not an exact parallel to today's combination of al-Qaeda operatives (a smaller but no less committed cadre), affiliated networks, virtually networked like-minded followers, and homegrown violent extremists. But the 1993 warning of an unstructured network of jihadists moving on from their current area of operations to other battlefronts could have been written this morning.

SECTARIAN PROXY WAR IN THE LEVANT

The Syrian war is also a classic case of a proxy war, in this case between Saudi Arabia and other Sunni gulf states, on one hand, and Iran, on the other, with the additional, especially dangerous overlay of sectarianism. The sectarian vocabulary used to dehumanize the ''other'' in the Syrian war is deeply disturbing and suggests both sides view the war as a long-term battle in an existential, religious struggle between Sunnis and Shiites.[31] This suggests further that the war in Syria is now being fought on two parallel planes, one focused on the Assad regime and the Syrian opposition, and the other on the existential threats the Sunni and Shiite communities each perceive from one another. The former might theoretically be negotiable, while the latter almost certainly is not. The ramifications for regional instability are enormous, and go well beyond the Levant. But they are felt more immediately and more powerfully in Lebanon to the west and Iraq to the east than anywhere else.

Allow me to focus briefly on Lebanon in particular. Over the past couple of years, Hezbollah's combatant role in Syria has become more formal and overt. At the same time, intercommunal violence has increased significantly in Lebanon, including gunfights between Sunni and Alawite militants in Tripoli, between Sunnis and Shiites in Sidon, and of course bombings by Sunni militants—including Jabhat al-Nusra in Lebanon—in Shiite neighborhoods in Beirut and Hermel. Hezbollah's stronghold in the Dahiya suburb of Beirut has been struck on multiple occasions, and even the Iranian Embassy in Beirut was the target of a double suicide bombing.

By siding with the Assad regime, its Alawite supporters, and Iran, and taking up arms against Sunni rebels, Hezbollah has placed itself at the epicenter of a sectarian conflict that has nothing to do with the group's purported raison d'etre: "resistance" to Israeli occupation. One Shiite Lebanese satirist put it this way: "Either the fighters have lost Palestine on the map and think it is in Syria," he said, "[o]r they were informed that the road to Jerusalem runs through Qusayr and Homs," locations in Syria where Hezbollah has fought with Assad loyalists against Sunni rebels.[32]

The implication is clear: for many Lebanese, Hezbollah is no longer a pure "Islamic resistance" fighting Israel, but a sectarian militia and Iranian proxy doing Assad and Ayatollah Khamenei's bidding at the expense of fellow Muslims. And it therefore does not surprise that the pokes come from extremist circles, too. In June, the Abdullah Azzam Brigades, a Lebanon-based al-Qaeda-affiliated group, released a statement challenging Hezbollah chief Hassan Nasrallah and his fighters "to fire one bullet at occupied Palestine and claim responsibility" for it. They could fire at Israel from either Lebanon or Syria, the statement continued, seeing as Hezbollah "fired thousands of shells and bullets upon unarmed Sunnis and their women, elderly, and children, and destroyed their homes on top of them."[33]

But while taunts might be expected from radical Sunni extremist groups, Hezbollah now faces challenges it never would have anticipated just a few years ago. For example, the day before Nasrallah's August speech Lebanese President Michel Suleiman called, for the first time ever, for the state to curtail Hezbollah's ability to operate as an independent militia outside the control of the government.[34] By sending fighters to Syria, many Lebanese believe Hezbollah has put its interests as a group ahead of those of Lebanon as a state, something that flouts Hezbollah's longtime efforts to portray itself as a group that is, first and foremost, Lebanese. Now the group that describes itself as the vanguard standing up for the dispossessed in the face of injustice, and that has always tried to downplay its sectarian and pro-Iranian identities, finds those assertions challenged over its refusal to abide by the Lebanese Government's official position of noninterference in Syria. To the contrary, its proactive support of a brutal Alawite regime against the predominantly Sunni Syrian opposition undermines its long-cultivated image as a distinctly Lebanese "resistance" movement.

Hezbollah has doubled down in its support for the Assad regime, even after bombs started going off in Dahiya, in southern Beirut. Nasrallah was crystal clear: "If you are punishing Hezbollah for its role in Syria, I will tell you, if we want to respond to the Dahiyeh explosion, we would double the number of fighters in Syria—if they were 1,000 to 2,000, and if they were 5,000, they would become 10,000." Indeed, Hezbollah—and Nasrallah himself—has cast its lot with Assad to the end. "If," Nasrallah added, "one day came, and required that Hezbollah and I go to Syria, we will do so."[35]

At one point, Nasrallah tried to paper over the fact that Lebanese Shiites and Lebanese Sunnis were now openly battling one another in Syria, and threatening to drag that sectarian fighting across the border into Lebanon, by proposing that Lebanese Shiites and Sunnis agree to disagree over Syria. Addressing Lebanese Sunnis, Nasrallah said in a speech last May: "We disagree over Syria. You fight in Syria; we fight in Syria; then let's fight there. Do you want me to be more frank? Keep Lebanon aside. Why should we fight in Lebanon?"[36] But that pitch did not go over so well with Nasrallah's fellow Lebanese, who wanted an end to Lebanese interference in the war in Syria, not a gentleman's agreement that Lebanese citizens would only slaughter one another across the border.

In that same speech, Nasrallah addressed the "two grave dangers" facing Lebanon. The first, he argued, is "Israel and its intentions, greed, and schemes." The second danger, Nasrallah added, is related to "the changes taking place in Syria." As for Israel, Nasrallah warned that it threatens Lebanon every day. And as for Syria, the regime there faces an "axis led by the United States which is for sure the decisionmaker." The British, French, Italians, Germans, Arabs, and Turks are involved, too, but "all of them work for the Americans." But the true force behind the "changes taking place in Syria"? "We also know that this axis is implicitly supported by Israel because the U.S. project in the region is Israeli cum laude."

Hezbollah is not fighting in Syria as part of a sectarian conflict, Nasrallah insisted, but combating a radical Sunni, takfiri project with ties to al-Qaeda that "is funded and backed by America" out of an American interest to destroy the region. In other words, the war in Syria is no longer a popular revolution against a political regime, but a place where America is seeking to impose its own political project on the region. Nasrallah concluded: "Well, we all know that the U.S. project in the region is an absolutely Israeli project." And so, by fighting in Syria, "today we consider ourselves defending Lebanon, Palestine, and Syria." [37]

There are, however, few takers for the contorted logic that the Syrian rebellion is an American or Israeli scheme outside Hezbollah's staunchest Shiite supporters. And the proportion of Shiites in Lebanon has fallen considerably since the war in Syria began. There are now as many as an estimated 1 million mostly Sunni Syrian refugees who have fled to Lebanon, marking a significant shift in the sectarian balance of a state whose confessional political system is based on a sense of proportional representation (albeit outdated) among its confessional communities. This has, to say the least, exacerbated sectarian resentment.

TRENDING TOWARD INSTABILITY

The humanitarian crisis resulting from the Syrian civil war is a catastrophe that grows worse by the day. In a region long known for its instability and sparse resources, Syria's neighbors are simply not equipped to handle 2.4 million registered refugees. Lebanon has taken in Syrians equal to at least one-fifth of the country's population, a refugee camp is now Jordan's fourth-largest city, and 13,000 new refugees are registered with the Office of the U.N. High Commissioner for Refugees (UNHCR) every day. Within Syria itself, more than 6.5 million have been displaced and more than 9 million need humanitarian assistance.

Such numbers are more than just a depressing snapshot of the situation on the ground today, they suggest a long-term outlook that is no less dire. Taken together, the Syrian crisis and its secondary and tertiary effects create a set of "looming disequilibria," to borrow a phrase from the National Intelligence Council's (NIC's) excellent study "Global Trends 2030: Alternative Worlds." [38] Consider, for example, the combined impact on the region of a years-long conflict, exacerbated by sectarianism and fueled by funds and weapons from the backers of respective proxies. From education, health, poverty, and migration patterns to humanitarian assistance needs and the economic impact on fragile economies, the consequences of the Syrian war for the region would be massive even if the war itself ended tomorrow.

Let us focus for a moment on refugee migrations, which have long been noted as factors that increase the likelihood of militant disputes. [39] In today's migration displacements, the vast majority of refugees are Sunni Muslims, posing a serious threat to the sectarian balance of the region, especially in Lebanon. Hundreds of thousands of Syrians have moved into Jordan's cities and put a heavy strain on local economies. Neither country can sustain for long the added burden to public services, from water and electricity to health care and education. This stress can open doors for externally financed terrorist organizations to take the place of the state, as was the case with Hezbollah in Lebanon in the 1980s. Without considerably more international aid, the entire region could well be facing increased instability and opportunities for extremists for the foreseeable future. Indeed, according to one study, "hosting refugees from neighboring states significantly increases the risk of armed conflict." Refugee camps provide militant groups with recruits and supplies, and refugee flows include within them fighters, weapons, and radical ideologies. Then there are the financial and social burdens on the host country, including disruption to the local economy and upsetting of the local society's ethnic balance. In the case of Syria, these researchers found, refugee influxes to Lebanon raise its risk of civil war by 53.88 percent, and raise Jordan's conflict risk by 53.51 percent. [40]

CONCLUSION

There is no question that the ongoing, deeply sectarian proxy war in Syria will undermine regional stability in ways both predictable and not. This testimony did not even touch on Iraq, Turkey, or Israel, for example, all of which are neighboring countries deeply affected by the war in Syria.

Even before the war in Syria got as bad as it has, projections for the region suggested we were headed in this general direction. I leave you with a quotation from the NIC's "Global Trends 2030":

> Chronic instability will be a feature of the region because of the growing weakness of the state and the rise of sectarianism, Islam, and tribalism. The challenge will be particularly acute in states such as Iraq, Libya,

Yemen, and Syria where sectarian tensions were often simmering below the surface as autocratic regimes co-opted minority groups and imposed harsh measures to keep ethnic rivalries in check. In [the] event of a more fragmented Iraq or Syria, a Kurdistan would not be inconceivable. Having split up before, Yemen is likely to be a security concern with weak central government, poverty, unemployment and with a young population that will go from 28 million today to 50 million in 2025. Bahrain could also become a cockpit for growing Sunni-Shia rivalry, which could be destabilizing for the gulf region.

And yet, I doubt anyone could have anticipated the catastrophe we now face in Syria, and the instability that is the result of the regional spillover from that conflict.

I submit that the United States is not doing anywhere near enough to address these critical problems. Failure to respond effectively to this crisis has led to tangible and horrific consequences today. Failure to quickly reassess our policies and roll out a far more proactive stance toward both the humanitarian crisis and the conflict itself will have equally damaging and painful consequences tomorrow.

I thank you for your attention and look forward to answering any questions you may have.

Notes

[1] The author would like to thank Jonathan Prohov and Kelsey Segawa for their research assistance in support of this testimony.

[2] "Worldwide Threat Assessment of the U.S. Intelligence Community": Hearing before the Senate Select Committee on Intelligence, United States Senate, 113th Cong., 2nd. Sess. (January 29, 2014) (statement of James Clapper, Director of National Intelligence), http://www.intelligence.senate.gov/140129/clapper.pdf.

[3] U.S. Department of State, Bureau of Intelligence and Research (INR), "The Wandering Mujahidin: Armed and Dangerous," Weekend Edition, August 21–22, 1993, available at http://www.washingtoninstitute.org/policy-analysis/view/globalized-jihad-then-1993-and-now.

[4] "Current and Future Worldwide Threats to the National Security of the United States": Hearing before the Senate Armed Services Committee, United States Senate, 113th. Cong., 2nd. Sess. (February 11, 2014) (statement of James Clapper, Director of National Intelligence).

[5] David Rohde, "Analysis: Is Syria Now a Direct Threat to the U.S.?" Reuters, February 7, 2014, http://www.reuters.com/article/2014/02/07/us-syria-us-analysis-idUSBREA161NG20140207.

[6] Aaron Zelin, "Up to 11,000 Foreign Fighters in Syria; Steep Rise among Western Europeans," ICSR Insight, December 17, 2013, available at http://www.washingtoninstitute.org/policy-analysis/view/up-to-11000-foreign-fighters-in-syria-steep-rise-among-western-europeans.

[7] David Horovitz, "5,000 Hezbollah Troops in Syria, with 5,000 More Set to Join Them," Times of Israel, May 26, 2013, http://www.timesofisrael.com/5000-hezbollah-troops-in-syria-with-5000-more-set-to-join-them/.

[8] Jamie Dettmer, "Number of Shia Fighters in Syria Could Rise Following Fatwa," Voice of America, December 16, 2013,http://www.voanews.com/content/number-of-shia-fighters-in-syria-could-rise-following-fatwa/1811638.html.

[9] U.S. Executive Order 13572, "Blocking Property of Certain Persons With Respect to Human Rights Abuses in Syria," April 29, 2011, http://www.treasury.gov/resource-center/sanctions/Programs/Documents/13572.pdf.

[10] U.S. Department of Treasury, "Treasury Designates Iranian Ministry of Intelligence and Security for Human Rights Abuses and Support for Terrorism," press release, February 16, 2012, http://www.treasury.gov/press-center/press-releases/Pages/tg1424.aspx; U.S. Department of Treasury, "Treasury Sanctions Syrian, Iranian Security Forces for Involvement in Syrian Crackdown," press release, June 29, 2011, http://www.treasury.gov/press-center/press-releases/Pages/tg1224.aspx.

[11] "Terrorist Groups in Syria": Hearing before the House Committee on Foreign Affairs, Subcommittee on Terrorism, Nonproliferation, and Trade, United States House of Representatives, 113th. Cong. (November 20, 2013) (statement of Mr. Phillip Smyth), http://docs.house.gov/meetings/FA/FA18/20131120/101513/HHRG-113-FA18-Wstate-SmythP-20131120.pdf; Ariel Ben Solomon, "Report: Yemen Houthis Fighting for Assad in Syria," Jerusalem Post, May 31, 2013, http://www.jpost.com/Middle-East/Report-Yemen-Houthis-fighting-for-Assad-in-Syria-315005.

[12] "Clapper Says Syrian al-Qaida Wants to Attack U.S.," Washington Post, January 29, 2014,http://www.washingtonpost.com/politics/clapper-says-syrian-al-qaida-wants-to-attack-us/2014/01/29/46f35732-8905-11e3-a760-a86415d0944dlstory.html.

[13] Michael R. Gordon and Mark Mazzetti, "U.S. Spy Chief Says Assad Has Strengthened His Hold on Power," New York Times, February 4, 2014, http://www.nytimes.com/2014/02/05/world/middleeast/us-representative-to-syrian-opposition-is-retiring.html.

[14] Jack Khoury, "Israeli Arab Gets 18 Months for Trying to Join Fight against Assad," Haaretz, February 11, 2014,http://www.haaretz.com/news/middle-east/.premium-1.573552.

[15] Glen Carey, "Saudis Fearing Syrian Blowback Expand Rehab for Jihadis," Bloomberg, December 9, 2013, http://www.bloomberg.com/news/2013-12-08/jihadis-offered-rehab-as-saudis-seek-to-avert-syria-war-blowback.html.

[16] Patrick Markey and Tarek Amara, "Insight: Tunisia Islamists Seek Jihad in Syria with One Eye on Home," Reuters, November 18, 2013, http://uk.reuters.com/article/2013/11/18/uk-tunisia-jihad-insight-idUKBRE9AH0GO20131118.

[17] Ibid.

[18] David Barnett, "Blowback in Cairo: The Syrian Civil War Has Now Reached the Heart of Egypt," Foreign Policy, January 9, 2014, http://www.foreignpolicy.com/articles/2014/01/09/blowbacklinlcairolsyria.

[19] Mohannad Sabry, "Al-Qaeda Emerges amid Egypt's Turmoil," Al-Monitor, December 4, 2013, http://www.al-monitor.com/pulse/originals/2013/12/al-qaeda-egypt-sinai-insurgency-grow- inginfluence.html.

[20] Vish Sakthivel, "Weathering Morocco's Syria Returnees," PolicyWatch 2148 (Washington Institute for Near East Policy, September 25, 2013), http://www.washingtoninstitute.org/policy-analysis/view/weathering-moroccos-syria-returnees.

[21] Ahmed Rasheed, "Militants Kill 16 Iraqi Soldiers in Overnight Ambush," Reuters, February 11, 2014, http://www.reuters.com/article/2014/02/11/us-iraq-violence-idUSBREA1A1BC20140211; Loveday Morris, "Shiite Militias in Iraq Begin to Remobilize," Washington Post, February 9, 2014.

[22] Loveday Morris, "Shiite Militias in Iraq Begin to Remobilize," Washington Post, February 9, 2014; Aaron Y. Zelin and Phillip Smyth, "The Vocabulary of Sectarianism," Foreign Policy, January 29, 2014, available at http://www.washingtoninstitute.org/policy-analysis/view/the-vocabulary-of-sectarianism.

[23] "Jordan Foils Bid to Smuggle Ammunition from Syria," Naharnet, February 24, 2014, http://naharnet.com/stories/en/1199555.

[24] U.S. Department of State, "U.S. Designates Gulbuddin Hekmatyar a Terrorist," February 19, 2003, http://iipdigital.usembassy.gov/st/english/texttrans/2003/02/20030219165118pkurata@pd.state.gov0.704632.html#axzz2t7LhTkjK. "The List Established and Maintained by the 1267 Committee with respect to Individuals, Groups, Undertakings and Other Entities Associated with al-Qaida." United Nations, January 6, 2014, http://www.un.org/sc/committees/1267/pdf/AQList.pdf.

[25] U.S. Department of State, Bureau of Intelligence and Research (INR), "The Wandering Mujahidin: Armed and Dangerous," Weekend Edition, August 21–22, 1993, available at http://www.washingtoninstitute.org/policy-analysis/view/globalized-jihad-then-1993-and-now. 69[26] U.S. Department of Treasury, "Treasury Designates UK-Based Individuals, Entities Financing Al Qaida-Affiliated LIFG," February 8, 2006, http://www.treasury.gov/press-center/press-releases/Pages/js4016.aspx.

[27] "Ansar al-Sharia Aid Campaign: For Our People in Bilad al-Sham #3," Al-Riyah Media Foundation, February 9, 2014, http://justpaste.it/ecxu.

[28] U.S. Department of Treasury, "Treasury Targets Networks Linked to Iran," February 6, 2014, http://www.treasury.gov/press-center/press-releases/Pages/jl2287.aspx.

[29] Tim Lister, "Al Qaeda 'Disowns' Affiliate, Blaming It for Disaster in Syria," CNN, February 4, 2014, http://www.cnn.com/2014/02/03/world/meast/syria-al-qaeda/; Aaron Y. Zelin, "Al-Qaeda Disaffiliates with the Islamic State of Iraq and al-Sham," Policy Alert (Washington Institute for Near East Policy, February 4, 2014), http://www.washingtoninstitute.org/policy-analysis/view/al-qaeda-disaffiliates-with-the-islamic-state-of-iraq-and-al-sham.

[30] Yaakov Lappin, "3 East Jerusalem al-Qaida Recruits Arrested, 'Planned Massive Bombings,' " Jerusalem Post, January 22, 2014, http://www.jpost.com/Defense/3-al-Qaida-recruits-arrested-planned-massive-bombings-339002.

[31] Aaron Y. Zelin and Phillip Smyth, "The Vocabulary of Sectarianism" Foreign Policy, January 29, 2014, available at http://www.washingtoninstitute.org/policy-analysis/view/the-vocabulary-of-sectarianism.

[32] Sarah Birke, "Hezbollah's Choice," New York Times, August 6, 2013,http://latitude.blogs.nytimes.com/2013/08/06/hezbollahs-choice/.

[33] Thomas Joscelyn, "Online Jihadists Discuss Fate of al Qaeda Operative Held by Saudi Arabia," Long War Journal, June 27, 2013, http://www.longwarjournal.org/archives/2013/06/onlineljihadistsldis.php.

[34] Anne Barnard, "Pressed on Syria, Hezbollah Leader Urges Focus on Israel," New York Times, August 2, 2013, http://www.nytimes.com/2013/08/03/world/middleeast/under-fire-on-syria-hezbollah-leader-urges-focus-on-israel.html?lr=0.

[35] Ali Hashem, "Nasrallah Threatens to Double Hezbollah Forces in Syria," Al-Monitor, August 16, 2013, http://www.al-monitor.com/pulse/originals/2013/08/nasrallah-double-forces-syria.html.

[36] "Hezbollah Leader Hassan Nasrallah's Speech on Syria," Voltaire Network, May 25, 2013, http://www.voltairenet.org/article178691.html.

[37] Ibid.

[38] Office of the Director of National Intelligence, "Global Trends 2030: Alternative Worlds" (National Intelligence Council, December 2012), http://www.dni.gov/files/documents/GlobalTrendsl2030.pdf.

[39] Idean Salehyan, "The Externalities of Civil Strife: Refugees as a Source of International Conflict," paper presented at the conference on Migration, International Relations, and the Evolution of World Politics (Princeton, N.J., Woodrow Wilson School of Public and International Affairs, Princeton University, March 16–17, 2007), http://www.cas.unt.edu/idean/RefugeesWar.pdf.

[40] Idean Salehyan and Kristian Skrede Gleditsch, "The Syrian Refugee Crisis and Conflict Spillover," Political Violence @ a Glance, February 11, 2014, http://politicalviolenceataglance.org/2014/02/11/the-syrian-refugee-crisis-and-conflict-spillover/.

The CHAIRMAN. Well, thank you both for some very insightful and alarming testimony.

Let me ask you both. You got to a little bit of this, Dr. Levitt, at the end there of your statement. If you were in a position to prescribe policy, what would you say? Both of you, what would you say it should be? Why do we not start with you?

Mr. GARTENSTEIN-ROSS. I clearly have the more minimalist view of what we can accomplish at this point. To me, I do not think we are going to be able to make an enormous difference on the battlefield in Syria, so I divide policy in two different ways. One is containing the impact of the spillover. That is reducing the amount of foreign fighters who go to the battlefield, making sure that we can track them, and reducing the humanitarian costs of the war.

But I think that above all else we have to actually commit to a policy. We should not be on the fence between regime change and something else. I think we need to make a choice. I take a more minimalist view. I understand that many colleagues have a very different view than I do in that regard.

The CHAIRMAN. Dr. Levitt.

Dr. LEVITT. Thank you. I completely agree with Daveed and some of the things we need to do, but I also think that, especially on foreign fighters, control of the border with Turkey, but I think there are other things we need to think really carefully about. How do we deny the Assad regime complete control over air? That does not have to be our boots on the ground. It does not have to be providing MANPADs to sketchy characters. We have other allies in the region. There are things we should be thinking about doing creatively in that area.

I think at a certain point we need to consider things that were on the table at one point when we were talking about a redline some time ago, that we do not necessarily need to escalate things too far. For example, it is my understanding that there are only 15 to 20 runways in the entire country of Syria that are capable of taking the massive airplanes delivering resupplies from Iran and Russia both directly to the Assad regime and Hezbollah and their allies. We have specialized munitions to take out those types of runways. There are all kinds of complications with this, but if we were able to do that then the consequence for the day after would be that they would not be able to get the kind of weapons resupplied that they are using on a daily basis to create this humanitarian catastrophe.

The CHAIRMAN. I think both of you referenced the challenge of those foreign fighters inside of Syria, who then return to their countries or elsewhere. Obviously, if you could take one of your policy suggestions, which is to control the borders and therefore avoid foreign fighters from coming in, you have one part of your answer. But how do we deal with the question of returning foreign fighters? In essence, are we looking at what is happening in Syria with al-Qaeda groups active in Syria, Iraq, and Lebanon? Are they in essence a JV team getting ready for varsity play?

Mr. GARTENSTEIN-ROSS. It is going to be a variety of answers. Some people go over, do not necessarily go to the front line, and are drawn there for emotional reasons. Some people do not even link up with jihadist factions. Others do. So the question for those who do is, Are they ideologically radicalized or is this something that they can be reincorporated, which is a tremendous problem for some of the countries in the region, especially those who have legal regimes where going over and fighting is not against the law? That means that they do not have the option of simply arresting. They generally try to monitor, but there are all sorts of people who have gone over who are not necessarily on their radar screen, which creates an intelligence problem. So I think the United States can be very helpful to partner nations.

Dr. LEVITT. As the chairman is aware, I recently published a book on Hezbollah. As I was going about talking about this, I had an opportunity to meet with senior intelligence officials around the world where this problem is going on. Different countries have different ways of dealing with it, from freezing people's passports to even denying citizenship, that we would not have here in the United States.

Here in the United States, this is a massive problem for FBI and DHS, trying to keep up. We have around 50 people who have gone, reportedly. They are not necessarily getting more full-time employees or more budget, but they need to keep tabs on every one of these people. And by the way, it is not just ISIS or Jibhat al-Nusra. People who are going to fight with nondesignated, not yet designated groups, like Al-Sham, are also a significant problem.

One of the things officials told me abroad is that they are seeing increasingly, because Syria is not seen as an offensive jihad—it is a defensive jihad—people are told: Look, the West is not going and defending these Sunni women and children, so we have to do it for our own. But when they get there, most of these people who go, the foreign fighters, end up fighting with the more extreme elements and they do, I am told by these intelligence officials, come back far more radicalized, not all of them, as Daveed said, but the vast majority do. And that creates a tremendous problem.

The CHAIRMAN. One final question. How much of the current activity in Syria, in Lebanon and Iraq reflects strategy guidance or operational directions from the Pakistan-based al-Qaeda from your perspectives?

Mr. GARTENSTEIN-ROSS. That is an excellent question. It is difficult to know, in part because we are trying to interpret what kind of guidance might be given by an organization that tries to keep its guidance hidden from view. We can see a few areas in which we can interpret them I think fairly well. We can see public messaging, for example, for which the Syrian jihad is really put at the forefront of the rhetoric coming out of al-Qaeda's senior leadership.

AQSL, al-Qaeda senior leadership, tends not to become as operationally involved, that is micromanaging things on the ground. Instead, the model that they have tended to use has been centralization of strategy and decentralization of implementation. So it would absolutely be a shock if we found that Zawahiri was, for example, directing operations on the ground in Syria.

One final thing I will note, where we can see the guidance coming from the broader al-Qaeda network. It was referenced in the previous panel by Director Olsen, the kind of tensions that currently exist, where the Islamic State of Iraq and Al-Sham was kicked out of the al-Qaeda organization. Subsequent to the assassination of an al-Qaeda figure, Al-Siri, one of the groups on the ground which is al-Qaeda-affiliated, Jibhat al-Nusra, put an ultimatum down after which it planned to attack ISIS. You had a number of al-Qaeda-affiliated clerics come out and condemn the ultimatum, after which Jibhat al-Nusra did back off.

This is something which is an indication of when the organization and members who are part of its organs act to try to influence an outcome in a certain way, it does make an impact. Again, that is not to say that they are micromanaging tactics. But you can see the influence of strategic guidance.

Dr. LEVITT. In a nutshell, I agree with everything Daveed said. I just would add this. You are now seeing a very interesting situation where ISIS is arguably the most capable of the most extreme organizations on the ground in Syria and it has broken with al-Qaeda. And when al-Qaeda core told it to stop it, they said: Forget you. So it will be very interesting to see if this leads eventually to the downgrading of ISIS or to the downgrading of al-Qaeda's brand, either of which could happen.

Al-Siri, who Daveed mentioned, who was assassinated, was affiliated not with Jibhat al-Nusra or with ISIS, but with Al-Sham, and his assassination was another message that they are not really taking the al-Qaeda core leaders' message very, very seriously. I think that what we are going to see from here and from Syria going forward is the proliferation of affiliates and nonaffiliates without necessarily seeing al-Qaeda core disappear. As I said in my statement, you have al-Qaeda core raising funds for Jibhat al-Nusra and others in Kuwait, in Qatar, some of that money being funneled through Iran with Iran's knowledge—it does not get much more complicated than that.

The CHAIRMAN. Well, thank you both for helping the committee in its further understanding of the challenges in Syria. With the appreciation of the committee, this record will remain open until the close of business tomorrow and the hearing is adjourned.

[Whereupon, at 1:30 p.m., the hearing was adjourned.]

ADDITIONAL MATERIAL SUBMITTED FOR THE RECORD

RESPONSES OF DEPUTY SECRETARY WILLIAM BURNS TO QUESTIONS SUBMITTED BY SENATOR BOB CORKER

Question. There is undoubtedly overlap between human rights abusers in Russia and those engaged in violating Ukraine's territorial integrity. Should the Magnitsky list be expanded to include these individuals?

Answer. We will continue to use the Magnitsky Act to sanction individuals who meet its criteria, including those who commit gross violations of human rights.

On March 17, President Obama issued a new Executive Order (E.O.) under the national emergency with respect to Ukraine that finds that the actions and policies of the Russian Government with respect to Ukraine—including through the deployment of Russian military forces in the Crimea region of Ukraine—undermine democratic processes and institutions in Ukraine; threaten its peace, security, stability, sovereignty, and territorial integrity; and contribute to the misappropriation of its assets.

This new authority expands upon E.O. 13660, which the President signed March 6, by authorizing the Secretary of the Treasury, in consultation with the Secretary of State, to impose sanctions on named officials of the Russian Government, any individual or entity that operates in the Russian arms industry, and any designated individual or entity that acts on behalf of, or that provides material or other support to, any senior Russian Government official. We have fashioned these sanctions to impose costs on named individuals who wield influence in the Russian Government and those responsible for the deteriorating situation in Ukraine. We stand ready to use these authorities in a direct and targeted fashion as events warrant.

Given that we already have the authority to target persons, including Russians, who are engaged in violating Ukraine's sovereignty and territorial integrity, we do not believe it is necessary to expand the Magnitsky Act criteria. Doing so could distract from the intended purpose of the act, which was to highlight human rights abusers within the state of Russia.

Question. DIA Director Lieutenant General Flynn testified that while chemical weapons stockpiles currently remain under regime control, the "instability in Syria presents a perfect opportunity for al-Qaeda and associated groups to acquire these weapons or their components." How concerned are you about this possibility?

Answer. We are aware of the risks associated with the security situation in Syria, and we continue to monitor Syria's proliferation-sensitive materials, as we have throughout the ongoing conflict. We assess that the Asad regime remains capable of maintaining the safety and security of its chemical weapons agent and precursors while they remain in Syria. We have been clear that the best way to reduce any risk of proliferation is for Syria to comply promptly with its obligations under U.N. Security Council Resolution 2118, the relevant OPCW Executive Council decisions, and the Chemical Weapons Convention. Syria needs to ensure a successful handoff of these materials to the international community at the Port of Latakia, so that they can be destroyed outside of Syria.

The United States and the international community have provided extensive material assistance through the OPCW–U.N. Joint Mission to ensure that Syria is able to safely and securely transport these materials, and the regime has demonstrated its capacity to do so over the recent weeks. While we cannot fully discount the possibility of an extremist group in Syria seeking to acquire chemical weapons agent or precursor, both the Syrian Opposition Coalition and the Supreme Military Council have publicly indicated that they support the elimination mission and have pledged to cooperate with the OPCW–U.N. Joint Mission. We continue to work with the OPCW–U.N. Joint Mission to ensure that CW materials are removed from Syria as safely and expeditiously as possible.

Question. In the absence of greater American or international involvement, what do you believe Syria will look like in 3 years? In 5 years? Is that a situation that we can reasonably contain? How can we prepare for a decade of instability caused by the Syrian conflict?

Answer. In my testimony, I highlighted four serious risks to our national interest posed by the current conflict—the risk to the homeland from global jihadist groups who seek to gain long-term safe havens; the risk to the stability of our regional partners, including Jordan, Lebanon and Iraq; the risk to Israel and other partners from the rise of Iranian-backed extremist groups, especially Lebanese Hezbollah fighting in Syria; and the risk to the Syrian people, whose suffering constitutes the greatest humanitarian crisis of this new century. On the current trajectory, all of these risks will be exacerbated over the next 3 to 5 years and it will be increasingly difficult to contain spillover from the conflict.

While we pursue a diplomatic solution, we are putting in place the elements of a long-term response to this protracted crisis—reducing the threat posed by terrorist networks in Syria, pushing hard against Iranian financing and material support to its proxy groups in Syria and elsewhere, intensifying our efforts to strengthen Syria's endangered neighbors, and supporting global efforts to ease the humanitarian crisis in Syria and the region.

To help mitigate the security and humanitarian challenges, the Department of State and USAID are providing more than $260 million in nonlethal assistance to support Syria's moderate opposition. The U.S. Government is also the single-largest donor of humanitarian assistance for those affected by the crisis, providing more than $1.7 billion in aid—nearly $878 million to support those inside Syria, and nearly $862 million to support refugees fleeing Syria and assist host communities in neighboring countries.

In FY 2015, we have requested $155 million to advance a political transition, counter violent extremism, support communities in liberated areas to maintain basic services and compete with extremist groups, and preserve U.S. national security interests in the region. The FY 2015 request also includes $1.1 billion for the ongoing humanitarian response in Syria and the region—more than 11.7 million people have been affected by the crisis to date, a number which is likely to continue to rise over the next several years.

We are clear-eyed about the fact that this conflict poses significant challenges for U.S. security and those of our partners. There is no doubt that sustained U.S. engagement and attention, in concert with our international and regional allies, will be required.

RESPONSE OF ASSISTANT SECRETARY DEREK CHOLLET TO QUESTION
SUBMITTED BY SENATOR BOB CORKER

STEADFAST JAZZ

Question. In November 2013, NATO held its largest live-fire military exercise since 2006. The exercise, called Steadfast Jazz, involved over 6,000 NATO troops but the U.S. contribution was only 160 personnel. Why was the U.S. contribution so meager?

Answer. The purpose of STEADFAST JAZZ 2013 was to certify the Joint Force Headquarters and component headquarters for NATO Response Force (NRF) 2014. Because the United States does not provide the Joint Force Headquarters any of the component headquarters, or a major ground element to NRF 2014's Immediate Response Force, a larger contribution would have been inconsistent with the exercise's primary purpose. STEADFAST JAZZ 2013 was combined with a command post exercise in the Baltic States, and although approximately 6,000 NATO troops participated in both exercises, the STEADFAST JAZZ ground live-fire portion was relatively small, and only a few hundred allied military personnel were involved. STEADFAST JAZZ 2013 marked the first time that a U.S. ground unit participated in a NRF certification exercise, and also marked the first time that a unit based in the United States deployed to train in Europe since the REFORGER exercises of the early 1990s.

www.ingramcontent.com/pod-product-compliance
Lightning Source LLC
Chambersburg PA
CBHW081141290526
45795CB00006B/2321